7/98
20

24
12|4|00

D1260367

Bollingen Series XIX: 2

LECTURES
ON THE
I CHING

CONSTANCY
AND CHANGE

RICHARD WILHELM
Translated from the German
by Irene Eber

BOLLINGEN SERIES XIX:2
PRINCETON UNIVERSITY PRESS

299.5128
W

Published by Princeton University Press, Princeton, New Jersey
In the United Kingdom: Princeton University Press,
Guildford, Surrey

ALL RIGHTS RESERVED

THIS IS PART TWO OF THE NINETEENTH IN A SERIES OF WORKS
SPONSORED BY BOLLINGEN FOUNDATION

Published in German as *Wandlung und Dauer*
Eugen Diederichs Verlag, Düsseldorf and Cologne, 1956

ISBN 0-691-09902-2
ISBN 0-691-01872-3 (pbk.)

Clothbound editions of Princeton University Press books
are printed on acid-free paper, and binding materials are
chosen for strength and durability

Printed in the United States of America by Princeton
University Press, Princeton, New Jersey

Contents

Translator's Preface

I first translated these essays many years ago, while still in graduate school. None of my fellow students knew German well, and the few who were interested in the *I Ching* in those days found Wilhelm's lectures a welcome guide. Encouragement to undertake the translation came initially from my teacher and mentor, Professor Ch'en Shou-yi. His guidance and support while preparing an initial version of this translation remain a vivid memory, and I wish to acknowledge my profound gratitude for his inspiring and unsparing help.

Much time has passed since our first introduction to the intricacies of *I Ching* thought. While I was on sabbatical at the Center for Chinese Studies at the University of Michigan in Ann Arbor, Professors Albert Feuerwerker and Rhoads Murphey suggested I submit the manuscript for publication. To both I wish to express my deep respect and thanks, for without their encouragement the manuscript would have continued to gather dust. The financial aid of a postdoctoral research grant at the Center for Chinese Studies enabled me to begin editing and revising the earlier version. I am deeply grateful to the Center staff for preparing and typing the revised manuscript. Special thanks are due Ros Daly for her patient and careful help with small and large technical details, as well as her expert advice on all matters concerned with the completion of the manuscript.

To Professor Hellmut Wilhelm I owe a lasting debt of gratitude. He carefully and painstakingly corrected and improved the translation to conform to the spirit of his father's thinking. Professor Wilhelm, furthermore, traced most of the references to Goethe's poetry, as well as references to Chinese texts. His numerous suggestions are incorporated in the footnotes. Any shortcomings that remain are my own.

The format of Richard Wilhelm's work has been faithfully preserved. His footnotes to the text, noted alphabetically, appear at the bottom of the page. My footnotes, numbered consecutively, are placed at the end of the text. Goethe, the thinker, is much in evidence throughout the essays. Unfortunately, neither the published version of his poetry nor the several literal renditions in the text does justice to Goethe, the poet. For this reason, and on Professor Wilhelm's suggestion, the German original of the poems was retained in the translation. In only a few places was Wilhelm's style modified for the sake of greater clarity and readability. The Chinese term Tao, which Wilhelm consistently translated with "Sinn," but for which no English equivalent suggests itself, was rendered as Tao.

Introduction

China and the Chinese have fascinated Westerners for several centuries past, and materials about the country and its people appeared in Europe in increasing quantities from the seventeenth century on. There were travel books, such as *Novus Atlas Sinensis de Martino Martini*, published in 1655, or more serious attempts, such as Athanasius Kircher's *China Monumentis . . . Illustrata* of 1670. Although the latter seems more a pictorial encyclopedia, it had wide currency among literate Europeans, and was soon translated into other languages. Histories of China appeared that were mainly inspired by reports from Jesuit missionaries in Peking. Two such histories were Le Comte's *Nouveaux Mémoires sur l'état présent de la Chine* in 1696, and the more ambitious four-volume undertaking by Du Halde, *Description géographique, historique, politique et physique de l'empire de la Chine . . .* in 1735. Not a few men wrote fondly about China, whether they had seen the country or not. And those who described it sight unseen let their fancy roam freely.

From the seventeenth century also date the first translations of Chinese philosophical works, undertaken by the Jesuits in China. There is a 1662 translation of the *Great Learning* (*Ta-hsüeh*), a 1687 translation of the *Doctrine of the Mean* (*Chung-yung*), and a 1687 translation of Confucius. Aside from the work generally attributed to Confucius, the first two are associated with Confucianism, and the ideas conveyed drew admiring comments from many an educated European. Confucian China was a land of marvels, as shown in the histories, and of wisdom, as shown by the translations.

Scant attention was paid to other Chinese classics, and their translation into Western languages began only toward the end of the nineteenth and beginning of the twentieth century. Among these, the *Book of Changes (I Ching)* was no more than mentioned in Jesuit reports. Thus, Father Bouvet, writing from Peking to the philosopher Leibniz (1646-1716), described the *I Ching*'s trigrams and hexagrams, and probably also sent Leibniz an arrangement of the hexagrams. Leibniz responded enthusiastically to the mathematical implications of diagrammatic representations of philosophical ideas.

Today, some centuries later, translations of Chinese works are readily available. So are histories of all kinds, travelogues, diaries, and memoirs. The name of Confucius is familiar in the West. Experts, and laymen as well, can speak knowledgeably about this or that aspect of China. Some people may still endow the land and its people with a tinge of exoticism, others may both fear and admire the great giant of Asia. But no longer is China a land of the fabled and mysterious.

Among philosophical works translated from Chinese, the *I Ching* has become quite popular in recent years. The work is available in German, French, and English translations, including two refurbished nineteenth-century English versions. Its popularity is an interesting phenomenon, and one is tempted to search for the causes in such familiar developments as the youth culture, radicalism, escapism, preoccupation with the esoteric, and resurgent interest—

academic or not so academic—in witchcraft and magic. Still, no matter how mystically or scholarly inclined a person may be, he cannot simply settle down to a reading of the *I Ching* and hope to understand it. The text is more often than not obscure; it refers to matters that are incomprehensible; it suggests symbols from another time and place; the language is terse and befuddling; and there is no unified and systematic exposition of a comprehensive world view. The list could be prolonged. Moreover, the book is a puzzle—even if a tantalizing one—not only to Westerners. According to one Chinese authority, no Chinese scholar for the past two thousand years can honestly claim to have understood the *I Ching*.[1] And yet in China the book has been a perennial favorite with many an educated and even not so educated gentleman. Should one conclude then that people anywhere, tenaciously or perversely, read that which they do not understand?

Not quite. To be sure, the *I Ching* text is complex and obscure. Still, its very abstruseness suggests an intriguing richness of multiple meanings. To explore the many facets of the book, therefore, Chinese and Western commentaries abound. In China, these have appeared for centuries down to modern times. In the West, literature about the *I Ching* is of fairly recent date, but only few works can be considered both scholarly and serious. Much of it is, one might say, simplistic, though it should not be judged too harshly. By their very nature, such writings have served to enhance the mystique and popularity of the *I Ching*.

Richard Wilhelm's German translation of the *Book of Changes* appeared in 1924. Although he had included numerous explanatory notes in the text, for years thereafter he lectured extensively to amplify the

work further. As an extremely careful translator of
an inordinately difficult book, Wilhelm was superbly
qualified to speak and write about the *I Ching*.
Moreover, because to him the text's scholarly dimen-
sions intertwined with the purely human, his lectures
and essays are a useful introduction to the book itself.
The essays in this volume are, therefore, a guide, as it
were, to a better understanding of this ancient work.

The four essays translated in this volume were initially given as several series of lectures between 1926
and 1929.[2] In these lectures, Richard Wilhelm
(1873-1930) expressed his reflections on the *I Ching*,
which he had worked on intermittently for eleven
years. Wilhelm's lectures are animated by a very distinctive spirit. Germany in the later twenties was polit-
ically and socially unstable, but intellectually exciting
and stimulating. It was a time of scholarship and art,
literature and music, and, above all, an openness to
other places and peoples. After the China Institute
was opened in 1925 in Frankfurt, Wilhelm maintained almost continuous contact with such well-
known figures as Martin Buber, Hermann Hesse, and
Carl Gustav Jung, all of whom had wide-ranging interests. How each may have influenced the other is
not important here. More important is the *Zeitgeist* of
an era. People of a certain time communicated on
matters of common concern, and their thinking, even
if momentarily, tended to go off in new and unexpected directions.[3]

Salome Wilhelm's biography of her husband,
Richard, suggests a warm and gregarious personality.
Although a prolific writer and translator, he was not a
retiring scholar, oblivious to the intellectual and political currents of his time. Hence the interpretations
apparent in these lectures convey as much about

Wilhelm, the author, as they do about the world in which he lived. The significance of these essays must be sought on two planes. They are the statements of a scholar who had a profound understanding of the *Book of Changes* and the Chinese cultural context of which it is a part. But they are also statements about the spirit of an era. As the twenties gave way to the thirties and forties, this spirit of often optimistic inquiry and interpretation disappeared in the madness of extremism and mass annihilation. Today, nearly fifty years later, both China and the world are vastly changed.

Hellmut Wilhelm, whose commentaries on the *Changes* are no less profound and important than those of his father, has remarked that Richard Wilhelm's "primary object . . . was to reproduce the *living* tradition of the book and its contents."[4] The emphasis that ideas must be related to living human beings, and that ideas as such remain alive when accepted, developed, and changed by others, appears to be a leitmotif in Wilhelm's life. It may be useful to sketch this in some detail.

Richard Wilhelm lived in China for more than twenty years. In the course of his educational work with the German mission in Tsingtao, and later while teaching in Peking, he was in contact with both Europeans and some of the major Chinese intellectuals of the early years of the twentieth century. He came to China not with narrowly defined missionary aims, but rather as a person broadly educated, with wide-ranging artistic and scholarly interests.

A predilection toward fine arts (repeatedly referred to in the essays), literature, music, sculpture, and especially the poetry of the great German writer

Johann Wolfgang von Goethe (1749-1832), had already appeared in 1891, the beginning of Wilhelm's student years. Never losing sight of these interests, he turned to the study of theology, and was ordained in 1895. After serving briefly as parish minister, Wilhelm went to China in 1899, under the auspices of the Allgemein Protestantischer Missionsverein. In Tsingtao, which had been under German control since 1897,[5] Wilhelm immediately began to study the Chinese language. From 1905 until his death, he produced a steady flow of translations, as well as articles and books on Chinese life and culture.

Wilhelm concluded his work with the Tsingtao mission in 1920 and returned to Germany. But in 1922 he was again in China, first attached to the German embassy, then as Professor of German literature and philosophy at Peking University. Though he would have preferred to remain in Peking, he returned to Germany two years later, when a sinological chair was established at the University of Frankfurt. Six years of tireless activity followed. He lectured widely, taught, translated, and wrote. A most significant achievement was the opening of the China Institute for the purpose of disseminating knowledge about China. The Institute also published an outstanding scholarly journal, *Sinica*, whose contributors (Speiser, Balasz, Eberhard, Forke, Kuhn, to name but a few) are well-known scholars in Chinese studies.

In 1913, with the aid of Lao Nai-hsüan (1843-1921), Wilhelm began translating the *I Ching*. Work was briefly interrupted at the outbreak of World War I, when Lao left Tsingtao, but was resumed upon Lao's return in 1916. The collaboration with Lao is significant.[6] He had obtained the *chin-shih* degree in 1872, after which he entered government service. A scholar of considerable repute, he was steeped in traditional learning. Unlike many others of his generation, whose views of China's classical writings were already undergoing subtle transformation, Lao's approach seems entirely traditional. To him, the Confucian texts as the carriers of Chinese values were living tradition and living authority. Through Lao, therefore, Wilhelm came to understand the *Changes* not as a book to be critically and "scientifically" studied, and, as happened later, to be reevaluated, but as a work rooted within the fabric of Chinese thinking. The distinction is important. Chinese scholars and intellectuals continued to read and examine the *I Ching* in the twentieth century, much as they had done earlier. However, insofar as their approaches to tradition were rapidly changing, their reading of traditional texts also changed. To read a text because it justifies all there is, and to read a text in order to find *whether* it justifies all there is, are two different activities. That Wilhelm infused his translation and interpretation of the *I Ching* with a living reality, as such communicable to the West, may in part, at least, reflect Lao's position.

Wilhelm's view of the *Changes* as an unassailably relevant work was reinforced by his interest in Confucius as a personality who had exerted tremendous (though often misunderstood) influence on both the *Changes*[7] and Chinese tradition. The latter is an undisputable fact. Still, it is noteworthy that even after Wilhelm's closer acquaintance in the early twenties with the more radical intellectuals at Peking University, his view was neither shaken nor abandoned.[8] His lectures in this volume furnish ample evidence.

In addition, however, it is quite likely that Wilhelm's interest in psychology, particularly Jungian psychology, led him to see the *Changes* as currently relevant. He discussed the psychological implications of the text at various times and within different contexts; and, of course, a careful reading of his notes to the hexagrams in the *I Ching* shows this view clearly. For example, he emphasized that the book's philosophy "penetrates more deeply from the conscious life of the human being into unconscious spheres . . . relaying a unified image of cosmos-soul experience. This transcends the individual, reaching mankind's collective existence." At another time, he addressed himself to the psychology of thinking, stating that the notion of true or false thinking is an erroneous one. Magic thinking, one of the bases of the *Changes*, when properly practiced, is as true as is logical-mathematical thinking. The system of *I Ching* thought, without being primitive, has captured and developed certain bases of primitive thinking that are now lost to the West. As to the linguistic implications, he pointed out that a word changes its meaning in relationship to other words. As related to one word, it may have one meaning, as related to another, its meaning will be different. Hence, concepts in the *Changes* are conceived as dynamic and therefore changeable.[9]

According to Wilhelm, the *I Ching* is as important to the West as it is to China. Many of the psychological insights of the *Changes* could be accepted by Westerners. They could lead to new ways of thinking about old problems. Thinking (not thought) as process, the dynamic element of words in association, and the relativity of concepts to thinking and words—all these were instructive and provocative in any context. Translating the text, then, was more than a scholarly task.

Wilhelm frequently expressed his concern for China and its monumental problems in the twenties. He was, however, also acutely aware of what he considered a crisis in the West. His was not what Joseph Levenson aptly terms a type of international *Schwärmerei*, but rather an attempt to understand how categories of thinking there and here can complement one another. In one of his essays he wrote that since the end of the nineteenth and beginning of the twentieth century, Europe and the world have been in mutual confrontation. Asia is within the world, and the problem for Europe is how to come to terms with the world. According to a Confucian view, there are four steps in social development, wrote Wilhelm. These are the individual, the family, the state, and mankind. The West had always emphasized the individual and the state. Individual development is extolled, and the single human being is regarded as central and as an atom of society. Overemphasis on the function of the individual has led to deterioration of the family. Unlike Westerners, the Chinese have given greater weight to family and mankind. The consciousness of the individual is contained in the family, and since traditional China considered itself the world, Chinese considered themselves responsible for humankind rather than for the state. China, of course, was neither the world nor all humankind, and, wrote Wilhelm in the twenties, China now no longer holds this illusion. The fact is, however, that society continues to be thought of as a large human organism, the strength of which lies in the family. When this view is compared with the Western notion of society as a mechanism of the state, where atoms are individuals, the question is not to choose one as preferable to the other. The question is rather whether the two views can be combined. And, if so, imitation or fashionable borrowing must be avoided.[10]

Individualism together with nationalism, the family together with humankind—neither is entirely good nor entirely bad. They are two different individual and collective self-images. Hence, the negation of individualism is as futile as is cultural borrowing. Instead, suggests Wilhelm, we should find alternative ways of thinking, that is, alternative attitudes, for he sensed that both in China and elsewhere cataclysmic changes were in the making.

Culture cannot be borrowed or mechanically mixed, according to Wilhelm, even if we eat caviar and drink coffee from different parts of the world.[11] Wilhelm was as attached to his particular past (that is, history and culture) as others were to theirs. It is intriguing to note the extent to which Levenson, for example, had similar misgivings when he cautioned against a "cultural esperanto." Culture cannot be created by "cultural selection boards," wrote Levenson, "taking the best from East and West for a nice synthetic balance."[12]

Still, each man had a vision, for each in his own way believed that China belonged within and was a part of the world. According to Wilhelm, "a comparison of different cultures will give us the possibility of recognizing the human basis and to elevate it to conscious awareness. This, together with the preservation of individual particularities, will become increasingly a source of strength."[13] According to Levenson, "I saw a world made when an understanding of Chinese history, without violence to its integrity and individuality, and an understanding of western history rein-

forced each other. The two histories belong together."[14] Both men asserted that we all participate in
the human condition (almost too trite to reiterate),
but neither Wilhelm in the twenties nor Levenson in
the fifties had the illusion of One Humanity.

Therefore, also, by explaining China and Chinese
thinking, Wilhelm was not motivated by the desire to
help an oblique cosmopolitanism, as he termed it, to
emerge. Instead, he envisioned a world of sharply delineated individuals (leading a specific life, "as do
plants in the forest"), without negating in difference
that which is held in common.[15] Although he described this common bond of humanity at times po-
etically, at times metaphysically, its conscious emergence and awareness was the result of practical and
painstaking work. As a scholar and translator,
Wilhelm conceived of his goals in the broadest possible terms.

Where are the origins of the *I Ching*? And wherein
lies the fascination of this complex and obscure work?
Surely, there are good reasons for the book to have
had a long line of commentators from the Chou dynasty on well into the People's Republic. Nor would
its current popularity in the West seem a mere fad.

Regarding the question of origin, according to
Chinese tradition, the formation and arrangement of
the *I Ching* text (that is, the text without the appendixes, the so-called Ten Wings) was the work of the
sage kings of antiquity. Chinese tradition probably
does not err in attributing multiple authorship to the
work. However, the form in which it exists today, experts believe, cannot be dated earlier than the Western Chou dynasty (1122-770 B.C.). And in its earliest
form it served the function of a diviner's manual.[16]

As such, the book contained linear signs that were

used as oracles. Possibly an unbroken line indicated a "yes" answer, a broken line "no." At which point the lines were combined into pairs and into more complex formations is uncertain. It is similarly uncertain whether the combination of lines into trigrams preceded those of hexagrams, or whether the trigrams were a later development. Moreover, the relationship of the original portions of the text to the linear representations is not entirely clear.

According to Hellmut Wilhelm, the earlier layers of the text, dating from the Western Chou dynasty, are no less beautiful or sophisticated than later additions. Both concepts and images were present, and the images were drawn from a large number of fields: mythology and poetry as well as what Wilhelm terms "archetypal configurations of specific moments in history."[17]

Although there is no reason to assume that philosophers around the time of Confucius (522-479 B.C.) were unacquainted with early versions of the text, it is listed among the classics (*ching*) only in the third century B.C.[18] By then commentary on the *I Ching*, which took the form of the appendixes, or Ten Wings, may already have been underway. Among the appendixes, the *Great Treatise* (*Hsi Tz'u Chuan*, or *Ta Chuan*) is the longest, and has been described as the most important. It forms the fifth and sixth Wing, and consists of a diverse collection of essays about the *I Ching*. The historian Ssu-ma Ch'ien (145?-90? B.C.) attributes this appendix to Confucius. However, textual and grammatical evidence suggests that it is a late Chou dynasty text. This attribution fits the context of third- and second-century B.C. philosophical and cosmological speculation, and supports the conclusion that new interpretations, consonant with current thinking, were needed.[19] As to the other appendixes, it is hoped that further researches will make more exact attributions, and, as a result, also elucidate the intellectual worlds in which they originated.

From the Han dynasty (206 B.C-A.D. 220) on, the *Changes* has continued as one of the most important philosophical works. Philosophers were inspired time and again to comment upon the meaning of the thoughts that the book contains, or to develop independent systems of speculation on its basis.

Even in the twentieth century, the *Changes* was not consigned to oblivion. The modern philosopher, Hsiung Shih-li (1885-1968), for example, used the book as a major source for developing his ideas, and some years ago, in the fifties and sixties, the *I Ching* was the subject of a major controversy in mainland China. A central issue, and obviously an issue of current concern, was whether the book contained traces of Marxian philosophy and the dialectic.[20] Although in the past few years discussion seems to have ceased, it is unlikely that the *I Ching* will disappear from view. Among recent archeological finds, hitherto unknown portions of *I Ching* materials have come to light.[21] And since, according to Chinese tradition, the *Changes* was one of several books spared when Confucian writings were burned in the Ch'in dynasty (221-206 B.C.), perhaps current discussions regarding the First Emperor of Ch'in will also lead to a new evaluation of the *I Ching*.

Still another and narrower tendency of *I Ching* studies should be noted. In the twenties and thirties, the book, together with the other classics, became the subject of critical and scientific investigation. Those scholars who engaged in what was called "putting the past in order" (*cheng-li kuo-ku*) read the *Changes* not because it affirmed truth, but to see whether it contained affirmable truth. Research into the meaning, significance, and function of the *I Ching* no longer recognized the book's position as a revered classic. Such scholars' work represented a decisive break with the traditional view that the book contains a living and authoritative heritage. Nonetheless, this research was important, for it created the foundation on which a disciplined study of the *I Ching* has become possible.[22] The work of the twenties and thirties led to successful attempts at more accurate dating of the various layers of the book and has, furthermore, focused attention on the variety of elements that make up the text.

Western scholarship concerning the *I Ching* has not been plentiful. There are still many unsolved problems. The major authority today is, without question, Hellmut Wilhelm. Thanks to his profound scholarship, many aspects of the various layers of the text are now more clearly delineated and defined. Like his father, he, too, has attempted to discern the broader philosophical elements of the *Changes*, and has concluded that "the system of the *Book of Changes* is the representation of a multi-dimensional world."[23] And within this world there is a pattern of constant and orderly change.

Aside from the various attempts to explain the *I Ching*'s numerological and theological system, mention should be made of C. G. Jung's theory concerning the book's divinatory aspects. As Jung sees it, the system of thought in the *Changes* is based on a principle that he terms synchronicity. Whereas causality, which is the basis of Western thinking, does not allow for the occurrence of chance (thus leaving its occurrence unexplained), synchronicity accounts for

chance happenings. It does so because it "takes the
coincidence of events in space and time as meaning
something more than chance . . . [that is, as] a peculiar
interdependence of objective events among themselves as well as with the subjective (psychic) states of
the observer."[24] In the sense that the *I Ching* proposes
an acausal technique for grasping reality—all reality
anywhere—it is another, more complete and all-
encompassing way of dealing with the world.

Even introductions need conclusions. If the *I Ching*
deals with the world, it also deals with life. And it also
deals with death. T'ao Yüan-ming, to whom Wilhelm
refers elsewhere in these pages, wrote his own
epitaph before passing on. In it, he expressed in
deeply moving words a part of the spirit that suffuses
the *Book of Changes*.

> . . . I have gone happily to draw water from the
> brook and have sung as I walked under a load
> of firewood. . . . As spring gave way to autumn, I
> have busied myself in my garden. . . . I have re-
> joiced in my books and have been soothed by my
> zither. Winters I have warmed myself in the sun,
> summers I have bathed in the brook.
>
> Men fear to waste their lives, concerned that
> they may fail to succeed. They cling to the days
> and lament passing time.
>
> Aware of my destined end, of which one can-
> not be ignorant, I find no cause for regret in this
> present transformation.[25]

Lectures
on the
I Ching

Opposition and Fellowship

═══════════════════════════════════════

If we want to understand the *Book of Changes* and its philosophy, we must begin with the fact that it was originally a book of oracles that answered "yes" or "no" to certain questions. An unbroken line denoted the "yes" answer, a broken line the "no" answer. But at a very early date Chinese thinking went beyond the mere oracle, and in the course of time developed this very simple method into a method of comprehending the world. While in Europe pure Being is taken as fundamental, the decisive factor in Chinese thought is the recognition of change as the essence. The Chinese position is a middle one between Buddhism and the philosophy of existence. Buddhism, which regards all existence as no more than illusion, and the philosophy of existence, which regards existence as real behind the illusion of becoming, are, so to speak, polar opposites. Chinese thought endeavors a reconciliation by adding the element of time. For when two incompatible conditions meet in time, they become compatible by following each other in time, the one changing into the other. This, then, is essentially the idea of the *Book of Changes*: opposition and fellowship are produced together by time.

But why is it necessary to assume opposites as a basis? Because practical experience teaches that everything we know moves in opposites. Indeed, the presence of opposites is necessary for experience to take place. There must be contrast between subject and object, for otherwise consciousness, or the knowledge of things, is altogether impossible; contrast between light and dark allows sense impressions to occur. Contrasts must exist for consciousness to be kindled. However, according to the *Book of Changes*, these opposites must not be regarded as enduring, but should be seen as changing states, which can pass from one into another. And because of this, contrast as such becomes relative. The point is merely to find the proper attitude for the understanding of contrast. By reaching such a position, a person no longer clings to one pole and assigns to the other a negative, opposite position, but, flowing with time, he can experience contrast itself. The stress here is on an inner adaptation to these outer opposites. If one maintains a harmony between the inner self and the surrounding world, the world, in spite of all diversity, can do no harm. This is perhaps Confucius' central contribution to the *Book of Changes*. Among China's sages, Confucius is described as the most timely. According to one of his statements, man's concern should not be to assume a fixed attitude that is forcefully maintained under any circumstances. An inflexible attitude naturally produces its opposite, perpetuating the battle. Since in accordance with this law of change, the moment of victory is also the moment of the turning point, neither side can achieve a conclusive victory. Rather, man should be in harmony with his surroundings; when prosperous, his conduct should be that of a prosperous man; when poor, his conduct should be that of a poor man; and when among barbarians, his conduct should be that of a man who is among barbarians. In this way every position in life is balanced by creating a harmony between the inner self and the surrounding world.

To create this kind of harmony, it is essential to find the proper position. And this proper position is in the center. Time, it was stated, is the necessary ingredient that enables us to experience opposites; and experience, in fact, is only possible if contrast is encountered. But we see now also the importance of not being borne along by time alone, for time cannot become reality, unless we have a resting point from which to experience it. As long as we are tossed and torn from moment to moment, reproducing a phantasy of our past in the imagination, or anticipating the future with fear and hope, we are merely objects among many such objects. Mechanically propelled by our fate, like all other purely mechanical objects, we are moved here and there by thrusts and counterthrusts. However, if we succeed in experiencing time, including its opposite from a central point of view, rather than withdrawing from it, then the circle will begin to close, and we can experience time as perpetuity. This consists precisely in time becoming harmonious. Only in this sense can we understand the statement from the *Doctrine of the Mean*, "Effect central harmony," a statement which, in fact, expresses the secret of the Confucian doctrine.[1]

In discussing the opposites recorded in the *Book of Changes*, we must first of all understand that they are wholly abstract. To be sure, individual images contain symbols, but behind each image we perceive an endless mirroring of reflections. I want to give only one example for such an image: the yin symbol. Yin may be the wife, but can also be the son; it can be the minister; and, under certain circumstances, it can be emotional elements as opposed to intellectuality. However, yin may also be the vegetative nature of our being, the anima as opposed to the animus. Inversely, it may be the masculine aspect in the woman, the aspect every woman contains within herself as a derivative. In short, it is always that element which is not primary, but somehow derived. Opposites are formed in this way. Relationships are present everywhere; fixed concepts are of no consequence, but the relationship of concepts—the functioning of concepts within which opposites move. Opposites provoke one another, and for this very reason they can be made to harmonize.

In the *Book of Changes*, T'ai Chi —— is represented as the basis of all existence. T'ai Chi is the Supreme Ultimate, the entrance into the phenomenon, the One, or, in other words, that something from which, as in the West as well, everything else is assumed to proceed. However, the secret that the *Book of Changes* expresses is that as soon as the One is established, its opposite is also created. Goethe said once that every emphatic statement immediately produces from within itself a contradiction. The case is the same here, for if the One is fixed in space by a line, its opposite appears. Now space is divided into an above and below, or when the line is placed horizontally, a right and left, or front and back. The sixfold extension of space, as it is termed in Chinese, is given with this one line and with its position. The establishment of this line results, furthermore, in the appearance of polar duality, which is the primary positive pole designated by an undivided (yang) line and the secondary negative pole designated by a divided (yin) line. Together with the originally established line, we obtain a triad as the basis of reality. Therefore, we read in the *Tao Te Ching*: "One produced two; two produced three; three produced the ten thousand things."[2]

The beginning of the phenomenal world is the establishment of these concepts. And no-action [*wu-wei*], which is important in Taoist thought as well as in Confucianism, is not quietism in our sense, but is the readiness to act the part in the phenomenal world assigned to man by time and his surroundings.

The possible combinations of the three divided or undivided lines is two to the third power, which equals eight, or $2^3 = 8$. Therefore, the *Book of Changes* uses, for all further illustrations of the energies that fashion reality, these eight possible, primary symbols, or basic trigrams (Pa Kua).

By designating the yang line as strong, and the yin line as yielding (respectively positive and negative), we obtain the following eight trigrams from their combinations.

The first trigram is Ch'ien, ☰, the Creative. The three undivided lines of Ch'ien are strong. Ch'ien, then, is the Strong, the Undivided, in which inheres the tendency to strive forward without deviating. K'un, ☷, the Receptive, with its three divided lines, is the opposite of Ch'ien. And if Ch'ien is considered as time, then K'un is space. Time is one-dimensional, and it always moves forward. For Ch'ien, the Creative, there is no backward movement, although the movement can stop. If it grows weak, it simply ceases, but as long as it moves, the movement is forward. K'un, the spatial, does not move, or rather the movement of K'un is an internal one. The motion is conceived as a self-division, and the state of resting is thought of as a self-closing. Hence, the movement of

K'un is never directed toward an object, but motion closed within itself.

These two principles, the Creative and the Receptive, are the basic opposites present in the world. God and nature, as Goethe would call it, although Heaven and Earth is a more familiar image with which to coordinate this pair of opposites. But we must always keep in mind that they are only images, in no way rigidly fixed, and they function as reference points for thoughts. Everything must constantly move, change, and remain fluid. And so, for example, one image can be spiritual, the other material; within spirituality one image can represent the intellectual aspect, the Creative, whereas the other may be the affective. There are endless perspectives, and the significance always lies in the relationship in which these trigrams may stand to each other.

Ch'ien, ☰, as the father and K'un, ☷, as the mother are coordinated with the six children. The mother now takes one line from the father, the Creative, and hence our first image is the oldest son, ☳, who accordingly resembles the mother. (In keeping with this idea, the sons take after the mother, and the daughters after the father. Of course, one could also speak of grandparents, and so on.) The second son is ☵ and the third ☶. The daughters are exactly the reverse of this. The oldest daughter is ☴, where the father principle is on top, and the crucial line is feminine. Next are the second daughter, ☲, and then the youngest daughter, ☱. Altogether we now have:

☰	Ch'ien, the Creative	☶	Ken, Keeping Still
☷	K'un, the Receptive	☴	Sun, the Gentle
☳	Chen, the Arousing	☲	Li, the Clinging
☵	K'an, the Abysmal	☱	Tui, the Joyous

The oldest son, Chen, ☳ , is volatile energy, the Arousing; electricity as moves, for example, in the ground at the beginning of spring.

This energy is transferred to a different area in the second son, K'an, ☵ . Now it is water and, to be specific, water in motion: "Toward Heaven it rises, from Heaven it descends, perpetually changing." It is the waterfall that rushes downward, is pulverized, rises high above again as clouds, and descends once more as rain. This is the Abysmal, that knows no limitations and unhesitatingly plunges into the depths. The movement is shown by one central active line, limited by two divided lines.

The movement reaches its boundary in the third son, Ken ☶ , Keeping Still, the Mountain. Here the strong line is above and the yielding ones below. The movement is oriented toward vegetation, for in China the mountain exists within a completely different conceptual context than in Europe. In China the mountain is seen as part of the surrounding world; as part of the forests, which grow on it; as part of the plants it permits to sprout; as part of the animals that reproduce upon it, and as part of the clouds, which are dispatched to supply the country with the necessary moisture. The mountain is considered as a center of life. And this is precisely the idea at the basis of Ken, Keeping Still. In this trigram the Heavenly is concentrated on earth, as it were—below the terrestrial and above the celestial—and therefore the atmospheric influences are drawn toward earth and life becomes harmonious.

The movement is similar in the three trigrams that represent the daughters. The first is Sun, the Gentle, Penetrating. The image here is the wind. Wind is that which penetrates into all grooves, and although it does not do so by force, wind is present everywhere because it is incorporeal. It may be of interest to compare Sun with its opposite trigram, Chen. Chen, ☳, is the electrically rousing, the thunder (we would say "lightning" in Europe, although both mean the same thing here), whereas Sun, ☴, is the intrusion of air. Sun tends more toward the material than Chen, and therefore the way in which it moves is also different, even though Sun too, is a very mobile element. It is not active, but in adapting itself is rather reactive. Sun clings, and being pliant, succeeds in its energetic efforts. Sun, for example, is also wood, the roots of which [as a tree] penetrate everywhere, and by attaching to everything bring up the life-sap from the earth.

The trigram Li, ☲, has a very interesting configuration. Here the strong lines are outside and the dark, yielding line is inside. The image is the flame, the Clinging. A flame cannot exist independently, for the flame can only be seen where there is combustible matter. We should observe how dynamically these processes are comprehended in Chinese thought. In Europe, elements such as fire were thought of as substances until only recently. There was the substance of air, the substance of fire, the substance of water, and the substance of earth. Such notions were prevalent throughout Europe. But in China fire is thought of otherwise. Fire is not a substance but an event, and its occurrence is based on its relationship to other things. The flame exists because wood is present. Therefore, clinging to something also means being based on something, hence, Clarity, Light. This once more is the opposite of K'an, ☵. And if we transfer the concept to cosmic realms, we see something unique. For now it is the sun that is dependent on Heaven. Although it is considered by us as the source of light, in China the sun is not thought of as primary.

Rather, it is a concentration of heavenly light; the light shining on the earth is concentrated in the sun. But the sun itself is dependent on the power of heaven. K'an is considered to be the moon within this framework. Correspondingly, there are in China concave mirrors that "bring the fire of the sun down," and convex mirrors that bring "the water of the moon down." (We are dealing here with a misconstrued natural occurrence, for, when on cool autumn nights a smooth mirror is pointed toward the moon, the water of the dew will naturally gather on it. And similarly, fire will gather on the reflector if it is pointed toward the sun.)

The movement culminates in the youngest daughter, Tui, ☱, the Joyous. Here the yielding line is above, and the strong lines are embellished by the yielding line. Tui symbolizes a smiling mouth, smiling and joyous, but although joyous, nonetheless imbued with melancholy. As a consequence there is another interesting relationship: Chen as spring and Tui as autumn. Autumn is joyous; it is the time of harvest, the time when the fruit of the field is brought home. But autumn, notwithstanding its joyousness, is also the time of judgment. Autumn is the beginning of death. Hence, concealed in this final, gilding joyousness is a certain severity; still hidden, but deep within already present. The symbol of Tui in nature is the lake—not the lake as water, but the lake as shining, mirroring phenomenon, such as the lake at the foot of the mountain (Tui is also associated with metal). Tui can also be vapors that rise from the lake and spread over the earth: non-mobile water, misty water, the lake, or the swamp. In other words, all those aspects of water that differ essentially from K'an, the symbol of active water. Tui is the resting, or reposing aspect of atmospheric water. Ken, ☶ , rests in the terrestrial realm, but obtains vitality through heavenly aspects. Tui, ☱ , in contrast, is the resting aspect of atmospheric water, which is made joyous by terrestrial affairs. These, then, are very characteristic opposites.

The eight trigrams found in the *Book of Changes* are arranged in differing sequences according to the views that govern them.

A suggestive meditation diagram, representing the process of life in its closed series of recurrent changes, is found in an old mantra in the *Shuo Kua*, Discussion of the Trigrams, Chapter II, section 5.[3]

The diagram here shows the cardinal points and hours of the day according to the European conception (north at the top).

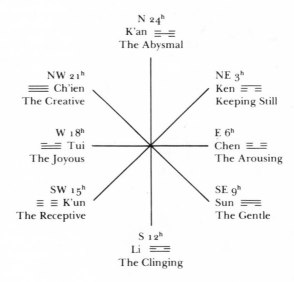

N 24ʰ
K'an ☵
The Abysmal

NW 21ʰ
☰ Ch'ien
The Creative

NE 3ʰ
Ken ☶
Keeping Still

W 18ʰ
☱ Tui
The Joyous

E 6ʰ
Chen ☳
The Arousing

SW 15ʰ
☷ K'un
The Receptive

SE 9ʰ
Sun ☴
The Gentle

S 12ʰ
Li ☲
The Clinging

This figure represents life as it unfolds in space and time. Space is designated by the cardinal points, and its sequence with the path of the sun represents the terrestrial development. As time itself changes, the spatial opposites follow each other, and eventually join harmoniously. Therefore, the eight trigrams are frequently coordinated with the day, and they can, of course, also be correlated with the course of the year. A cycle of twelve hexagrams from the *Book of Changes*, the so-called *P'i Kua*, is often also correlated with the course of the year. But it will not be cited here, for it is based on different principles, and involves different considerations.

These eight trigrams, then, are coordinated with the times of day and the cardinal points, and have, in addition, very interesting psychological correlations, which are important in this context. A correlation of psychological effects with the night hours as they follow one another is, for example, also found at the beginning of the second part of *Faust*. There, Faust, who is tired of life, is strengthened again through the vitalizing forces of the elves. Indeed, we find a most remarkable agreement of Goethe's concepts with those of the *Book of Changes* in this scene.

In order to observe the intrinsic workings of these spatial-temporal stages, we must understand fully that each of the eight stages takes three hours, with the climax of each at a given time in the middle. For example, the first stage lasts from 4:30 until 7:30, and the climax is at 6:00. This may be considered the ideal time for sunrise. Furthermore, these considerations necessitate that one position oneself in the center of the circle, looking toward the south. The movement that takes place from left to right should then become psychologically plausible.

According to the mantra, the individual stages are explained as follows: 1. "God comes forth in the sign of the Arousing." God is here understood as the expression of the newly awakened life energy. The trigram Chen, ☳, designates the moment at which life begins to stir anew. Pure strength is represented by the undivided, heavenly line below, whose function is to set the terrestrial into motion. The sun rises, morning slowly dawns, and things attain reality. At first, only psychic, innermost elements are awakened to life; the shell of sleep is cast off. But this casting off is the first budding connection with the outside world. And here, immediately, at the beginning of day, an act of conscious deciding must take place. For at the first movement of life, things are still far removed from us, but just because they are far we must influence the budding beginnings of the surrounding world in such a way as to permit only the approach of that which is suitable for us. The trigram, the Arousing, is very active. And the nature of its activity determines the way events of the surrounding world will take shape for us. Just like the sun, which begins its course like a hero determined to be victorious, we must consciously anticipate the victory of the daily battle and approach actively the day and its work, even though these are only the first beginnings, and everything is still in a process of germination.

2. Under the trigram Sun, ☴, we reach the next stage, which immediately shifts from the spontaneously subjective realm to the reactively objective realm. Here we read: "He brings all things to completion in the sign of the Gentle." Sun, the Gentle, represents the concept of penetration. Hence, its meaning here is that forms become actuality. When day awakens, life approaches and suddenly assumes real-

ity. Those individual demands in all their details, which we may have forgotten in the course of the night, approach again, and it is important now to fulfill them with vital energy. The more precise explanation reads, therefore: "Completion means that all creatures become pure and perfect." Things are once more infused with reality. It is a rather curious concept that objects lose reality at times, but acquire it again, when we, by projecting our interest upon them, give them reality, so that such objects become again of importance to us. The idea is psychologically very plausible. If we succeed in removing our entire interest from any one object, this object ceases to exist for us. It will disappear in the chaotic mass of collective existence, which to us is without relationships and accidental, and which we disregard. We can only give our attention to those objects with which we can establish a relationship by permitting something of ourselves to flow into them. In this way we construct ourselves, and as a practical consequence, our surrounding world, each day anew. What matters, therefore, is that we build our world with circumspection, and consider beforehand the type of interest we want to direct toward each thing. Our strength will have to be spent again and again. If the direction of our strength were to be reversed, as it were, the resulting blockage over a prolonged period of time would have ill effects. And so, we must choose sensibly the objects of our attention before they have come too close. If we procrastinate, or indeed, neglect to make a choice in time, then demands will be made on our attention, whether we had intended to give it or not. And such attention as is snatched from us while we watch passively is, as a rule, not harmonious. However, by preparing the beginning of the coming day in time, that is, when God comes forth in the sign of the Arousing, it is possible to make the day harmonious. In anticipation of this harmony we must also decide what we want to experience, and remain steadfast in our resolution to shape successive experiences so that they correspond to our nature and to our resolution. Although this attitude requires a certain lack of consideration, this lack is not an unfriendliness, but a strength-conserving position, helping to make one's energies effective toward positive ends.

Here, then, is the first contrast: the Arousing followed by the Gentle. The opposites are reconciled because of the time sequence, for it is within time that we first choose the things that are to occupy us later. Having once chosen, we can be effective without taking action, because we have beforehand determined how to allot our attention, and only that becomes real which is of value to us. Whatever is disturbing in our surroundings we relegate to the background. Should it be impossible to remove entirely such disturbing elements, and if we must deal with them, then we can prepare an approach of gentleness and not harshness. It is never possible to resolve unpleasantness with harshness; this merely concretizes the unpleasant. However, wind, the Gentle, is able to dissolve things. Do not the winds of spring melt ice because of their gentleness, while the storms of winter only make ice harder?

3. We have reached noon, when the day is at its zenith. This time of day stands under the trigram Li, ☲, the Clinging (Light). The *Book of Changes* says the following about Li: "He causes creatures to perceive one another in the sign of the Clinging (light)." "The Clinging is the brightness in which all creatures perceive one another. It is the trigram of the south. The

holy sages turned their faces to the south while they gave ear to the meaning of the universe, and through their clarity (brightness) everything became ordered."[4] Here things are beginning to relate to each other, here activity begins. But this is again a curious sort of activity, for it is activity based on contemplation. There are different ways and means one can use to deal with objects and men, and to recognize them. One way is to single out the characteristics of things, to draw conclusions from these singled-out characteristics, and by joining together the conclusions to reach judgments. This is the way of observation. However, another is the way of contemplation, of intuition, which is not altogether logical, although by intuition we understand a way that is supralogical and not opposed to logic. Intuition that contradicts logic is not truly intuition, but prejudice. Real intuition is in accord with logic, only it transcends logic. It is, so to speak, not dependent on the thin thread of deductive reasoning, but has a broader basis. And only on the basis of this type of intuition can effects be produced. Indeed, effectiveness only and always occurs when the inner life of the other person is also grasped. Exterior effects by means of terror are probably also possible, but such effects are only temporary phenomena. Force produces neither real nor lasting effects. Rather, the only lasting impact is produced by contemplation and understanding from within, and precisely, therefore, it can act in clarity upon the inner life of others. This is the principle of cultural creativity that Confucius accepted from the *Book of Changes*; a principle that will assuredly assert itself in the course of history in spite of momentary countercurrents.

4. After all things are clarified, we have the trigram

K'un, ☰ ☰, the Receptive, of which it is said: "He causes them to serve one another in the sign of the Receptive." K'un here does not have its cosmic significance, but is aligned in the psychological process and means fellowship. After subject and object assume a mutual relationship, mutual service in fellowship follows, and because of this all things are nourished and become complete in life.

Completeness of life is possible only in fellowship. No man can complete an enterprise alone and unassisted; the completion of any task demands such fellowship. The artist too, needs the community to complete a work of art; indeed, he perhaps more than anyone else. But fellowship does not necessarily mean that we associate with neighbor X or neighbor Y, in whose company we might find ourselves. Rather, fellowship can extend over centuries and millennia. And even if no one in our immediate environment offers such fellowship, nothing should prevent us from reaching back centuries or millennia into the past; there we can always find a stimulating relationship of fellowship, by means of which a given task can be completed. Confucius, during the time of his greatest loneliness, lived in just such fellowship with the Duke of Chou, although he was separated from him in time by five centuries.[5] However, it is not really necessary to go back this far. As a rule, in accordance with the type and the nature of work, companions will be found with whom the task must be and can be completed. In this connection the important point to realize is that such work is to render a service. All work is service, is responsibility. And precisely, therefore, the opportunity to work should be used as the opportunity to serve. As a result, we also should not be overly selective regarding the people with whom we are to work. We will be at fault if we cannot make anything of such people! Since we are contemplating man and are trying to comprehend his inner nature, we must learn to find a point of contact. Once this point is found, we can work together; a task will be accomplished and will mature.

5. We now have reached evening, with its very interesting contrast to morning. The daily work is in the process of being concluded. The various threads run together. Here we have the trigram Tui, the Joyous, ☱, of which it is said: "He gives them joy in the sign of the Joyous." The harvest of the day is brought in to be fashioned in joyousness. This process is also very important, for all productive work requires joy. Slowly, as the last threads run together, the accumulated dust of day must be shaken off. The time of dust is specifically associated with K'un. There are frictions and all sorts of difficulties; but after this dust has disappeared everything at last will radiate joy. Then only work will show itself as productive. "He gives them joy" (that is, God gives joy to all creatures) "in the sign of the Joyous."

The above trigrams represent the active part of life. And now we come to nighttime.

6. Although the night hours are entirely different, they are no less productive. The sphere of activity is completed, and now man reaches the trigram Ch'ien, the Creative, ☰, of which we read: "He battles in the sign of the Creative." But day is past and night has begun; what creative acts can now take place? Should we not assume that such acts properly belong to the beginning of day? The trigram Chen, the Arousing, is also a form of the creative; a form suited exactly to the day's work, but the Creative in this place has an altogether different meaning. Here it is written: "He

battles in the sign of the Creative." The work of day is done; with pleasure and joy things have been concluded. But now the question arises: has this day been of productive value, or was it a pretty emptiness? Hence the Creative, because now man must justify himself. Indeed, if one has responsibilities, they also require justification. The guardian of the threshold demands an answer from us, with yardsticks other than the superficial and social. A creative answer is demanded: are there in the harvest seeds germinating for a new task, or is it an end without further development? Just as November winds blow away and disperse all rot and decay, sparing only that which contains life and can blossom again next spring, so man, too, will do well to insert one serious moment before falling asleep. This one moment—it need not take long—should be a glance at the day, concerned with the essential meaning of this day. For this reason we read: "He battles with him." It is always a battle, when day asserts its rights in the face of God's judgment. Heaven is the Creative, or God; and man's success has to be won in opposition to God, although not the God who is conceived as something external, but God within us. This is the core of the issue. When I am done with my work, then I can battle with God within me. Even if despair and despondency make everything seem useless, provided I am consciously responsible, I can nonetheless assert myself against these inner voices. Thus Jacob, in the Biblical story, contended with the angel of God for his work, and even though the angel broke his hip, Jacob was victorious. Tseng Tzu, a disciple of Confucius, expresses this same idea when he says: "I examine myself daily in three ways."[6]

7. Now comes midnight. For this time we have the

trigram K'an, the Abysmal, ☵, of which it is written:
"He permits them to rest from their toil in the sign of
the Abysmal." The Abysmal in this place has a special
meaning, within which the moon is also significant.
This is life's night side, when day becomes incorporeal, and man collects the day's harvest in the abyss
of the subconscious. This process may take place in a
variety of ways. Some people, and most of us share
part of our psychic life with these, work on the surface. Whatever has been given shape on the surface
now collects in the treasure house of dreams. There it
will be effective as a dream; be reshaped and then assume the form in which it is conveyed into the subconscious. But does not Chinese wisdom tell us that
the greatest sage does not dream? This means that
the sage is able to do without the reactivating images
called dreams because his state of existence is such
that he can convey experiences directly into his innermost being. The innermost being is the line in the
middle—the line that flows between the two steep and
precipitous brinks: ☵. Life at this point withdraws
to a final center. Sleep has begun, and sleep extin-
guishes consciousness; this is the night, when no one
can effectively work. Now there is simply receptiveness. But not receptiveness standing still, for it still
has the stimulus from the life of the day. And if something valuable is present it goes on.

8. We have now come to the strangest time of all,
early morning. Its sign is Ken, the Mountain, Keeping
Still, ☶. Of Ken it is written: "He brings them to
perfection in the sign of Keeping Still," and "Keeping
Still is the trigram of the northeast, where beginning
and end of all creatures are completed." In China, the
northeast has a mysterious significance, being at once
the place of life and the place of death. Each city had

at one time a temple in which T'ai-shan, the great mountain in the northeast of China, was honored. Since this mountain was the place of contact for life and death, both births and deaths were announced in these temples. Transferred to the course of the day, this means the extinction of yesterday and the preparation for tomorrow. By observing a normal way of life, we can see that these early morning hours have enormously strong regenerative powers. To be precise, from these hours completely new currents of energy may be drawn. If we succeed in apprehending these energies, they will provide a supply for the coming day that will enable us to lead a very vigorous life.

Unintentionally, these expositions have led us from the day, as it unfolds in the course of twenty-four hours, to the day of life. And here we are permitted an insight into the Chinese way of thinking. Life is conceived as a day, a day that is gradually molded, finds its effectiveness, and that must vindicate itself, gather its fruits, and that eventually ends in this mysterious Keeping Still, when past and future touch one another. Confucianism does not give exact expression to what happens and how it happens when the mountain is reached. Life enters the mountain and comes forth from it again. Is it the same human being who has been reembodied, or is it another who has absorbed the ripened fruits of life, and has thus begun a new life? Confucianism is silent on this subject. Taoism, on the other hand, adopted the popular Buddhist notion of the transmigration of souls. Buddhism proper does not have the doctrine of transmigration as we understand it. For Buddhism acknowledges only states, and not substances—not even a soul substance. But no matter how we interpret this image, we can be certain that at the basis of these views is the problem of change. By entering into change, while continuing to maintain the center in change, it is quite possible to raise the transitory state to the state of eternity. Therefore, it is also possible to create a work that through evolution and subsequent involution contains a tension that causes the work not to cease with death. Instead, through this tension, a new cycle is set in motion. In this sense, man's task should be to lead a life that will give it this tension. The energies present in life ought to be so concentrated that when all externalities are shed, there will remain one actuality, one entelechy, which as monad somehow once more assumes shape, and for which it will become possible to enter upon further progress.

Opposition and fellowship complement one another; opposites are necessary for the individual to comprehend himself, and fellowship is necessary for the individual to find his sphere of activity. By complementing one another, a work that continues the past and passes something on to the future is completed. In this sense, what is to come is not mere illusion, and time does not merely elapse, but becomes *Kairos* [turning point, the moment of decision], meaningful time—that is, time capable of asserting the moment in reality when contrasted with eternity.

The cycle of contemplation closes with this secret, as expressed by Goethe in his own way in the poem "Symbol":[7]

> Die Zukunft decket
> Schmerzen und Glücke.
> Schrittweis Dem Blicke,
> Doch ungeschrecket
> Dringen wir vorwärts.
>
> Und schwer und ferne
> Hängt eine Hülle

Mit Ehrfurcht. Stille
Ruhn oben die Sterne
Und unten die Gräber . . .

Doch rufen von drüben
Die Stimmen der Geister,
Die Stimmen der Meister:
Versäumt nicht zu üben
Die Kräfte des Guten.

Hier winden wir Kronen
In ewiger Stille,
Die sollen mit Fülle
Die Tätigen lohnen!
Wir heissen euch hoffen.

Though weal and woe
   The future may hide,
   Unterrified
We onward go
   In ne'er-changing race.

A veil of dread
   Hangs heavier still.
   Deep slumbers fill
The stars overhead,
   And the foot-trodden grave.

The voice of the blest,
   And of spirits on high
   Seems loudly to cry:
"To do what is best,
   Unceasing endeavor."

"In silence eterne
   Here chaplets are twined,
   That each noble mind
Its guerdon may earn,   —
   Then hope ye forever!"

FROM OPPOSITION TO FELLOWSHIP

At this point more details must be added to the subject of "Opposition and Fellowship." I shall discuss, then, a constellation of hexagrams that I obtained for this year's meeting[8] in accordance with the ancient Chinese method. My reason for wanting to develop them here is that they seem to be especially applicable to the present world situation; a situation found in Germany as well as in China, in Europe as well as in America. All of us are living now in a period of opposition; it is important that we may hope for the transformation of opposition into fellowship. In fact, this is precisely the importance of the world-view described in the *Book of Changes*: there is no situation without a way out. All situations are stages of change. Therefore, even when things are most difficult we can plant the seed for a new situation that will preserve within itself the present situation, though we must be capable of adapting and of finding the proper attitude. New conditions, therefore, are never without affinities to a previous situation. Rather, that which is oppressive in the present situation will pass, and the situation will exist both in a preserved and transfigured state, just as "Opposition" is preserved in "Fellowship."

By using the hexagram before me, I would like to give an example of how the *Book of Changes* represents these hexagrams as "changing." The hexagram we are dealing with is "Opposition," and I would like to trace it back through the changes out of which it originated.[a]

[a] Partly for the sake of simplicity, and partly for other reasons, the Chinese commentaries do not give details regarding the internal changes of the hexagrams (*Kua Pien*). In my translation I have

The first lecture dealt with the eight basic trigrams and their differences. Each one of the trigrams—and perhaps this was the original nature of the oracle— can be transformed into another. The first trigram, called Cheng, was as a rule written below, while Hui, the trigram into which it passed, was above. In this manner sixty-four hexagrams, consisting of six lines each, are obtained, and these make up the *Book of Changes* in its present form.

Let us examine one such hexagram: P'i, ☰☷, no. 12. P'i has the trigram Ch'ien, the Creative, above and K'un, the Receptive, below. Hence P'i should be a fairly good hexagram. But it is not. P'i is the hexagram "Standstill [Stagnation]." But how does standstill set in? Heaven moves upward, it rises; Earth moves downward, it sinks. Therefore, in this hexagram the movements of Heaven and Earth grow apart; the Heavenly withdraws ever farther upward, the terrestrial sinks downward, and as a result, a standstill in life is produced. For after all, life is based on mutual penetration of Heaven and Earth—the Creative and the Receptive—but this can only take place when the Creative is below and the Receptive is above. In that position all energies are working together, whereas in hexagram P'i they are working in opposition and against each other.

The hexagram of the standstill of life is the first discernible beginning of opposition. At one time or another in life a period of stagnation may set in, when life's energies, instead of acting in unison, will pull apart. At first, standstill is present in the cosmic sphere, or in the sphere of life itself.

----

followed this custom for the same reasons. However, even the old-est preserved commentary (*T'uan Chuan*), often attributed to Con-fucius, presupposes these changes. It might, therefore, be interest-ing for once to pursue this process.

Presently, however, in accordance with the law of change in time, the hexagram Wu Wang, ☰☳, no. 25, evolves from hexagram P'i. A strong line appears below, replacing the weak bottom line. This is the hexagram Wu Wang. Wu Wang is very peculiar, and its name is not easy to translate. I have used "Innocence," though it could also be the "Unexpected," or the "Unintentional." Having meanwhile thought about the matter more, I would today render Wu Wang with the term "Subconscious," even though this expression seems somewhat too modern. In any case, the meaning of Wu Wang has this connotation. That which as standstill severs life enters here into subconscious realms. It is not yet conscious. To understand this, we must necessarily consider still one more arrangement of the hexagram: the internal structure may also be divided into three groups of lines. A hexagram may be understood as consisting of two each of the eight basic trigrams. But once ordered, they may also divide as follows:

$$
\begin{array}{ll}
\text{═══} & 1 \\
\text{══ ══} & 2 \\
\text{══ ══} & 3
\end{array}
$$

Here the two lower lines are terrestrial or animal-vegetative; the two upper lines are heavenly, or spiritual; and the two middle lines represent man and his soul. Hence there is Heaven and Earth—the two poles of existence—with man as connecting link; or spirit and matter, and in this case living matter, as the two poles of human existence, and the soul as tie. Now on the very bottom, in material existence, a strong line appears, and causes a shock there, since this lower trigram is precisely Chen, ☳, the shock, the Arousing, thunder. Standstill now is transformed into internal shock, which does not yet enter consciousness. The Creative is without, and therefore, still can act forcefully, but security within has disappeared. Because the shock is within and is unconscious, it cannot take its course, and therefore causes the unexpected to happen. An unexpected disaster is afoot; something may be robbed or stolen, as it is explained in greater detail in the text to the hexagram.

This change however, is still not final, for now another curious development takes place. Two lines change places; the upper middle line takes the place in the middle of the lower partial trigram, and the weak middle line from below takes the place of the upper: ☲☱. The entire hexagram is reorganized, and we now have K'uei, "Opposition," no. 38. And while in Wu Wang the shock was internal, as if subconscious, here opposition appears in consciousness. This in turn can be explained by considering the composition of the hexagram.

Below is the trigram Tui, the lake, water that sinks downward: ☱. Above is Li, the flame that blazes upward: ☲; the trigrams are, therefore, in opposition. There is, however, still the internal arrangement of the hexagram that must be mentioned. Within K'uei are the so-called nuclear trigrams ☲ and ☵,[b] which are also interesting. K'uei is composed of two trigrams, the water of the lake below, ☱, and the flame above, ☲. But in the internal arrangement, one nuclear trigram, the flame, ☲, is below, and the water of the rain, ☵, is above, so that the movement of the water—from above downward—wants to extinguish the fire. Once more opposition. This hexagram therefore harbors internal opposition throughout its entire structure.

[b] These nuclear trigrams are the two trigrams which—by eliminating the lowest and uppermost line—intersect each other

These opposites appear now on the surface, and become conscious. The upper trigram is Li, Clarity. Li signifies clear consciousness or intellect. The trigram below is Tui, which is not only joyousness, but also speech. Now there will be "talk," and the intellect will begin to act. And so opposition can be expressed externally precisely when this internally torn and paradoxical structure is frayed by speech and logical thought.

The Chinese commentary points to one further condition. Although this condition does not fit European circumstances, I do want to mention it here for completeness' sake. Two sisters live in one house; the youngest sister Tui and the second sister Li. The oldest sister is not with them. Both dwell together in one house, but their temperaments are not in accord, and there are quarrels. However, some day they will both marry into different families and will be separated one from the other. Were the eldest sister present, the situation would not be one of opposition, for she would represent unequivocal authority. But such authority, which is instrumental in adjusting conflict within the family, does not exist to the same degree among the younger sisters. The conflict in this case can only be solved by the daughters' marriage, when they will become a part of their new families and subordinate themselves to the proper authorities, who will assign them their respective positions. Then the quarrel will be resolved by fellowship.[c]

The question posed now is, what is one to do in

---

in such a way as to share the two middle lines. With hexagram ䷥ , the complex of the nuclear trigram is, hence, ䷾ , which divides into ☵ above and ☲ below.

[c] It should be understood that the image of the two daughters is a relative symbol. Two classes, or divergent political tendencies, could also be assumed.

such a situation? For this situation is by nature dangerously susceptible to further aggravation. In national life a condition can arise in which the average energies, the broad energies of the middle class, become, as it were, frayed, and an extreme polarization toward the top and toward the bottom takes place. Political unity is lost, as it is actually taking place in national states throughout the world. Apparently nationalism, a stage of political development we have reached today, instead of joining together nations, even if only in mutual cohesion against other nations—which is certainly reconcilable with the concept of nationalism—is producing further contrasts and new cleavages. Thus each political party splinters into new parties, causing opposites to reach a proportion of disorganization so that ruin seems inevitable. This would be the result were the movement to continue forever.

But the movement does not continue. Eventually it reaches a point within itself where, in one way or another, it changes again. However, we see in the *Book of Changes* that change for the better is not motivated by a natural process, but by the presence of responsible individuals who will take charge of the situation. There must be individuals who, recognizing the difficulties, still dare act toward surmounting the opposites. Only a nation with such individuals can escape destruction. Otherwise the hexagram P'i takes effect; the nation falls apart, explodes as it were, and becomes fertilizer for new nations that grow on its ground. This too has happened in the course of history; such periods are always long, desperate, and unfruitful. Nations may be ruined to the point that they can be scientifically excavated, such as Babylonia or Egypt, but in the interval much time has passed, and this time brings naught but misery, destruction, and want. If we therefore were to assume the imminent decline of the West, which would be intimately connected with the decline of the Orient, or a decline of all humankind, then there is no country anywhere that could gladly say of itself: "We are in a better situation, the beginnings toward betterment are already present with us." And, therefore, we believe that here a situation confronts humankind which must by all efforts be overcome.

It is imperative that we look at this in two ways, because this situation cannot be solved from one point of view. Here we read: "Opposition means estrangement. The men of ancient times strung a piece of wood for a bow and hardened pieces of wood in the fire for arrows. The use of bow and arrow is to keep the world in fear. They probably took this from the hexagram of Opposition." This is the war-like aspect, forever present in situations of this nature. We read, furthermore: "In small matters, good fortune. Fire moves upward. The lake moves downward. Two daughters live together, but their minds are not directed to common concerns."[9]

Opposition cannot possibly be solved if one nation restores order in its domain and then subjugates the rest of the world. This was the idea of imperialism, which periodically convulsed humanity. The last of these occurred in the Mongol period, when a nucleus had assembled, then stormed through whole continents. But Genghis Khan's impulse, as such, had in the end no effect. To be sure, a last judgment seemed to have begun, and the surplus population of the world was decimated, making space for future generations; but order was not created. If something is to emerge from opposition, we simply cannot think of building a united Europe, or of marching against Russia and Asia in order to subjugate both. And here we are not even concerned with the interests of the United States of America. A united Europe can crystallize only in conjunction with other, simultaneously occurring crystallizations. The central problem of the issue is a world problem, the problem of the world as the cosmic power of life. The only solution to it is a concentration of various world centers, and the beginning of mutual relationships between them. Only such a solution will help overcome the present condition.

This makes it both harder and easier to cope with the situation. It is easier insofar as we naturally think first of all of our country—be it Germany or China—to know that others have the same difficulties and that we need not fear being late; there is still time for us as well as for the others. It is, however, bad that we as well as our hexagram are internally so disorganized, that the national reorganization presents endless difficulties. Without this national reorganization, nothing can be done; the concept of the nation, once having appeared, cannot be destroyed, just as we cannot abolish the concept of the individual. The day of rearing herds is past. And I do not hesitate to express the conviction that Bolshevist attempts to organize the Russian people once more into an amorphous herd[10] must fail principally because this rung on the ladder of human evolution has been passed. Once the individual has arrived, he cannot be negated; he must be accepted as he is in the new period. But this creates a difficulty. Obviously, the individual is in opposition to the character of the nation, and national individualism is, in turn, also in opposition to organized humankind.

How is a solution to be found? Solutions will be found when ideas become embodied in men. Ideas are always present, but they are impotent. Scheler is quite right when he speaks of the impotence of spirit.[11] Actually, this upper world has nothing to say deep down there; spirit has no ties, and is, indeed, very remote from material circumstances. Spirit and nature are separated by worlds, and spirit cannot directly influence nature. But spirit has a different kind of power; it has power over that strange being, which stands in between nature and spirit: the human being. Nature shares in man from below and by force, for we are all subject to the necessity of natural laws. The law of nature acts on us, and there is nothing we can do about it; it is necessity that acts. But, in addition, we are also more or less subject to the law of freedom of spirit that acts, not through force, but through goals, so that the ideal motivates human will:[12]

> Nehmt die Gottheit auf in euren Willen,
> Und sie steigt von ihrem Weltenthron!

> Take the divinity into your will
> And it will descend from the throne
> of the universe.

Here spirit is indeed effective, proving that it is, after all, not powerless. To be sure, spirit is impotent when having to deal with the lower aspects in man, but it is not impotent in men whose real sensitivity for the world above causes them to do more than look down and grub in the mire. And these are the men who count; with such men rests responsibility. There must be human beings who consciously affirm the natural law within, who are consciously modern with all the consequences this entails. Nothing deters such men; such men accept the entire past and whatever it contains, and they stand on its ground. Should they be unable to do so, then they have no power, are dissociated—are dreamers. And neither dreamers nor poets have ever changed the world. Men who change the world are men of reality, who stand on the ground of reality and its brazen laws. At the same time, their heads must reach into Heaven, and from there absorb cosmic powers. At first their personality absorbs these powers, but after points of concentration appear, or dynamic fields are opened, chaos becomes cosmos.

The movement of the lines from the hexagram "Opposition," no. 38, into hexagram no. 13, "Fellowship with Men," shows this process.

From ☰☱   To ☰☲
    Opposition   Fellowship with Men
    K'uei   T'ung Jen

Three lines have changed. And this change has caused a curious thing to happen: two lines have changed places—the middle line of the upper partial trigram moved down, and the lower, strong line moved up. From the surface of the earth that faces man, something moved upward to the lower side of Heaven, that is to say the side that also faces man. In this way Clarity, ☲ , above becomes Strength, ☰ ; while Joyousness, ☱ , below becomes Clarity, ☲ . Only the third line underwent a principal change.

Let us first take a closer look at this change; later we will look at the whole. The name of the first hexagram is "Opposition." However, Opposition as such contains one moment of order when, as yet not absolute, it can be dissolved. For this reason the text reads here: "Joyousness and dependence on Clarity." And, therefore, Opposition consists of Joyousness below, or within, and Clarity above, or without. "Within" and "below" are identical, as are also "without" and "above." "The yielding progresses and goes upward, attains the middle, and finds correspondence in the firm. This is why there is good fortune in small matters. Heaven and earth are opposites, but their action is concerted." Opposition exists as between idea and reality, between freedom and necessity; their effect, however, their effectiveness in man, is concerted. "Man and woman are opposites, but they strive for union. All beings stand in opposition to one another; what they do takes on order thereby. Great indeed is the effect of the time of opposition." This is positive opposition. Opposition prevents chaotic mixing. All life is organized, but only where contrasts are present can organisms arise. Therefore, disintegration, differentiation, into various functions always takes place simultaneously with the development of life. This is as true for the development of the human body as it is for the development of the human soul; and it is as true for the development of a political system as it is for the development of society. Individual spheres must increasingly separate out for the whole to encompass ever larger areas, which in turn organize. Opposition is necessary for organization. But opposition must not end in the disintegration of the organism; rather, strong internal ties must sustain the organism. Therefore, the explanation continues: "Above, fire; below, the lake: the image of opposition. Thus amid all fellowship the superior man retains his individuality." Therefore, we cannot have internationalism at the expense of nationalism; we cannot have a peace movement by painting over all opposition. We must acknowledge contrasts as given by nature, but dissolve them within a larger context.

This is not simple, and the subsequent difficulties are on the whole not understood. To begin with, a few individuals must be ready to undertake those first steps, for which they will have to experience that which all others who ever undertook first steps have experienced: they will be persecuted, ridiculed, and eventually forgotten. (And this is precisely the beauty of it; once they are forgotten, their work is accomplished.) Work is carried out in two ways. There must be men who can assume responsibility for their nations, but at the same time, each nation must have people who represent the other nations. There must be Germans, Frenchmen, Chinese, or Englishmen, who, in spite of clearly recognizing their own nations' deficiencies, affirm their nations. And because they are Germans, Frenchmen, Chinese, or Englishmen, they accept their destiny, their karma, and their heritage, and defend their nation. This is the meaning of "Right or wrong, my country," which does not mean that I will do everything, be it good or bad. But it means that I must take upon myself even the evil of my country, and when my country takes a course I must condemn, I will not part from it. Opposition within the nation is thus overcome. However, as long as we condemn others and are prepared to dissociate ourselves, the step that leads to surmounting opposition is not taken.

We must also have international "representatives." Such representatives have the duty to defend to the nations of the world the country assigned them by fate and experience, and to produce understanding where only misunderstanding exists. For example, at the present time, no peoples' innermost core is more misunderstood than that of the Chinese. Therefore, interpreters of the soul of China are needed, if humanity's coherence is not to be rent asunder. To be sure, a representative will suffer when, in critical moments, everything tends to develop contrary to human progress. But this precisely is his responsibility: internal worries must not lead to external condemnation, matters must be explained in the spirit of productive love, and everything will take a turn for the better. For there is no greater damage then when a so-called expert changes sides and condemns where he should love. Such burdens must be assumed and defended to the outside world. Only in this way will it be possible for nations to establish contact with each other. Representatives of individual nations must be prepared to give their lives to intercede, for the nation—the nation that has not been chosen at will, but which fate has assigned.

Let us now look more closely at the changes and movements of the hexagram K'uei, as well as what the text of the *Book of Changes* has to say about those moving lines. The following situations arise.

1. The second line moves first. By rising upward, as mentioned above, it changes from a strong into a yielding line. This is accompanied by the text: "One meets his lord in a narrow street. No blame." Quite an untimely event. A servant should meet his master, or a traveling statesman meet his appointed sovereign publicly when the assignment is received. But here the situation is such that no master is present, and the meeting is a clandestine event in a narrow street. All at once one looks beyond the chaos of the day and perceives what it is necessary to perceive, and this perception takes a sudden hold and obligates. It is a deep and entirely internal experience, and must be accepted internally. From now on, one should prepare to live or die in the service of this idea. This is

important, because everything created in heaven or on earth is created in blood, not, however, in the sense that each man who works for an idea must be literally crucified. It happens occasionally, but is always exceptional. Rather, in the sense that man's lower aspects—the second line belongs to earth, that is, necessity—accepts his karma, his fate, which from within the situation has been given him and which he affirms. The image of the narrow street indicates that this is not a simple transaction. A counterpart is, for example, found in the Bible, when a prophet receives his calling. Prophets are such men who have met their masters in narrow streets. How the prophet Jeremiah rages and complains! All his life he reproaches God for having burdened him with too heavy a load, but nonetheless accepts his destiny and completes the task. This experience deep within is by no means only pleasurable and great. At first we are altogether overawed by the burden of responsibility.

2. The next moving line is the third, which changes from a weak into a strong one. Here the difficulty is most intense. The line must change completely. It must change from a weak into a strong one, and thereafter will have no further connection to another line. And while previously I spoke of two who met and who had a relationship, here the relationship has ceased. A complete change is taking place. This, however, is connected with utmost difficulty. The accompanying text reads: "One sees the wagon dragged back, the oxen halted, a man's hair and nose cut off. Not a good beginning, but a good end." This is the time of battles. Often, just after receiving the call, one makes no progress. And even if one succeeds for a short time, obstructions soon develop. One's own person is seen as weak among so many strong persons,

and the movement, which is still governed by opposition that must be overcome, has at every step internal as well as external obstructions. Errors would seem to have crept into biographies of great men, when such men's lives are represented as internally unified. Especially erroneous is this concept when applied to the greatest of men; there is no personality complete within itself and capable of retaining its own clarity when confronted with the world of contradictions. Rather, these contradictions—when the wagon is confronted by an obstacle and the oxen are dragged back—cross over into one's inner nature in accordance with psychological laws. During the hours of night, during hours of loneliness, these contradictions rage in the soul. Therefore, the side of the soul turned toward mortal existence must be forged to hardness, and change from weakness to strength. This "depersonalization" (*Entwerden*) requires a dying, and this is the obstruction. A certain type of dying is required. One must consent to a complete reorganization of personality before acquiring the strength to act as the necessary agent capable of overcoming opposition.

This is the high point that frequently is more clearly enunciated by artists. Men of action must not show their struggle outwardly. They must settle things within, and reappear the following morning, as Jesus said, after such "fasting" with anointed head and washed face, as if nothing had happened, and not at all in doubt about the past experience. The artist, however, shows the experience while it is taking place. Let us take, for example, Beethoven's symphonies. Time and again, we find precisely in the greatest of these—the Eroica, the Fifth, or the Ninth—the point of differentiation, when opposition, the impossible, the superhuman, confronts the idea that comes from above and demands assertion. Forcibly one stops with a gasp, and a lament is wrested from the soul; for the moment one stands in awe and does not know how to continue before the onset of the turning point.

People who want to assume responsibility must undergo some part at least of such experiences. This cannot be spared us; it is our fate.

From this point of view, we now see a world of infinite multiplicity. There are, naturally, people who must act outwardly and in prominent places; there are, however, also others who act in quietude, of whom the public perhaps never hears. But this does not matter, for effectiveness has very little to do with what we call "the public." More important is that thoughts be thought clearly and strongly. Only a pure and absolutely sincere thought can be the seed, a seed planted in the ground. The carrier of the seed may disappear, he may be known or not—nothing is added to the situation either way. This is, for example, the unique aspect of Confucius' destiny. Throughout his life he tried to obtain a responsible position in order to contribute to the equalization of opposition. From beginning to end, life placed obstructions in his path; he was reviled and abused, "his hair and nose have been cut off." This means— and the image is a reflection of dishonorable punishment—that he was stigmatized, "he is the one who knows that a thing cannot be done and who keeps on doing it."[13] Yes, this abuse weighed on him. But his greatness consisted precisely in knowing that a thing cannot be done, and continuing to do it. Knowing that something cannot be done is simple, but still continuing to do it, this is the decisive contribution. And so Confucius pursued in absolute integrity his life's thought to its very end, and died without having seen the least trace of success. But success was there. And when the time came, the seedling that he had fashioned grew out of the earth, giving China durability for millennia to come. This seedling gave China the strength that has nourished it down to our time.

3. The last line to move is the fifth, which changes from a weak into a strong one. Here victory is already decided. The text says: "Remorse disappears. The companion bites his way through the wrappings. If one goes to him, how could it be a mistake?" Now we are above, in the sphere of Heaven, or in the realm of the spirit, and man has bitten his way through the wrappings. Hercules not only cleansed the Augean stables, but also bit his way through, and when he appeared among the gods, was greeted by Hera. Indeed, what blame could there be, what mistake, if one goes to him?

Man has finally reached the spiritual realm. Opposition is overcome, and the hexagram "Opposition" has changed into T'ung Jen, "Fellowship with Men," ☰☲. This hexagram is composed of Inner Clarity and Outward Strength. Opposition continues internally; it has not been destroyed, but it has been suspended. The text reads: "Fellowship with men in the open." These are not private associations, but are great, human associations. "Success. It furthers one to cross the great water." This is, so to speak, the transition into the cosmic realm. The ancient Chinese called the water in front of the sacred grove the "great water," and it was necessary to cross this water when entering the grove during the seasonal spring festival. Crossing the water meant entering the divine realm on earth, and thereby approaching the divinity. It is beneficial to cross the water. Great things can be undertaken, unheard of things become possible, and the unattainable is attained. Hence, the text comments: "The perseverance of the superior man furthers." Those same men who up to now have struggled with their oxen, and whose wagon was pulled backward; whose hair and nose seemed cut off, and who endured all sorts of obstructions, these same men now organize humanity and create a fellowship of men. And their communion has the stamp of uniqueness, and therefore signifies a time not of decline, but of ascent and of renewal.

I can no more than express the wish that the ideas contained in this old book will be restored in us, and that the prophecy—if we want to call it this—expressed by these words will come true. If this were the case, then the time of misery we are living in would not be hopeless, but would change into a time of fellowship. We alone will be to blame if it does not happen.

The Spirit of Art According to the Book of Changes

A number of hexagrams in the *Book of Changes* explain the spirit of art. I would like to reflect upon art from three points of view. Today, during our first evening, I want to discuss art of the imagination, under which I understand poetry and the plastic arts; tomorrow, the art of sensations, the Arousing in man's psyche and how it is fashioned; finally, the day after tomorrow, outwardly manifested art: the art of conduct, the art of fashioning life forms, and their results.

The hexagram Pi, Grace (*Book of Changes*, no. 22), ☲☶, stands for imaginative art, or song and image endowed with form.

Pi, to be properly understood, must be seen within the flow of change. Pi must not be considered constant;[1] it has developed from other hexagrams, and causes, in turn, further development. According to Chinese tradition, the hexagram T'ai, Peace (*Book of Changes*, no. 11), ☷☰, gave rise to Pi. T'ai is composed of the trigram Ch'ien below and trigram K'un above. Ch'ien is the Creative, Heaven, time, the internal, movement, the firm. K'un is the Receptive, Earth, space, that which enables forms to originate, the resting, the yielding.

Obviously, these two principles are joined together here in a creative event. The creative—Heaven—is below, the Receptive—terrestrial—is above. This reminds us of the holy symbol of the Altar of Heaven in

Peking. North of the actual altar is a rotunda of three stories, where it was customary to pray for a prosperous year. The rotunda is a living symbol of T'ai, showing how Heaven sank into Earth. Heaven is portrayed, on the one hand, by blue color, and on the other, by the symbol of the dragon—the invigorating power that penetrates the universe. Earth is portrayed by green color—because this is not simply ground, but organic earth—and by the phoenix. The phoenix, though he soars in Heaven, is born from Earth. In this holy place then, an interchange is portrayed: the dragon is nowhere displayed in the blue field; he is below, in the green field—Heaven below Earth! And the phoenix soars above, in the blue field. Earth is carried and surrounded by Heaven.

The movement of the elements in hexagram T'ai also portrays the union of the Creative and the Receptive. The Creative moves forcefully upward, the Receptive moves downward, and as their directions are toward each other, the two trigrams penetrate one another. Such also is the creative process in man. Every creative human being, who eventually fashions a work of art, has these two elements. He must have the Creative element, the temporal and masculine, as well as the feminine, the Receptive and spatial. Both are necessary for the idea to materialize and to become meaningful. A so-called incubation period is also necessary for the work of art to originate. "Veni Creator Spiritus"; Goethe once designated this song as representing to perfection the artistic creative process. Spirit comes and subordinates itself to soul, and by coming down and subordinating itself to the soul it permeates the soul, the soul conceives thereby, and the work of art is formed. The transformation of the hexagram T'ai into Pi represents this process.

☰☰ becomes ☰☰

This is shown symbolically by one line, the central line, as it detaches from the Creative below, and ascends upward. In hexagram T'ai the central line of the lower trigram changes into a yielding line, while the strong line moves to the very top of the hexagram.[d]

The ascent of the central line of the lower trigram to the top produces a tension, and this tension is precisely the motive through which the work of art is created. The two trigrams, the Creative and the Receptive, have now developed into two new trigrams: the lower trigram Li, is the flame, the sheen, the Clinging; and the upper trigram, Ken, is the mountain, Keeping Still, the Resting. Transferred to the human face, Li is the eye and Ken is the forehead; or, to be more precise, the point above the center of both

[d] Actually, we could also stipulate the ascent of the central line of the Creative, and its subsequent place as the central line of the Receptive. And, indeed, this hexagram occurs in the *Book of Changes*; it is listed next to the last, the hexagram "After Completion." The meaning is obvious. When all energies are equalized, and all tension is suspended, an end is reached and a state "After Completion" ensues, which presupposes no further developments. Each line is in its place—strong lines in strong places, weak lines in weak places—and any stimulus for creating a work of art is gone. Therefore, because of the unproductivity of the hexagram "After Completion," the sages who arranged the *Book of Changes* in its present form were not content to place it at the end of the book. Once more they dared attempt a reversal, and to recombine the lines—strong lines in weak places and weak lines in strong places—producing the hexagram "Before Completion." Only in this way is continuation possible. The conclusion is not final, but its direct counterposition, the opposite of the conclusion, is final! A sudden transposition develops "After Completion" into "Before Completion," with further possibilities for development.

eyes. A curious analogy is occasionally found in the West. Not long ago, while discussing with a painter the creative process she experienced, she told me: "When I have nearly completed the conception of a picture, I experience at first a state of restlessness. I feel full of energies, I am excited and receptive, but it is so to speak, a chaotic state. Then suddenly a crystallization process begins; the image sits in between the eyes, and once the image is there I can begin to paint and the painting will be a success. All doubt vanishes and only the technical problem remains of how to transfer onto the canvas what has gathered up here." How strangely, indeed, the creative process of the *Book of Changes* coincides with the artistic experience still found today in Europe. If furthermore, the spirit of these halls[e] were questioned, we would find the recurring notation in his diaries that his whole being is concentrated between his eyebrows. And such remarks always resulted from especially productive moments, when he was agitated by the need to fashion that which had already taken shape within him.

In answer to what consequences such a position will have for the spirit of the work of art, Confucius has said: "The firm ascends and gives form to the yielding. The yielding descends and permits the firm to give it form." The firm central line of the lower trigram ascends and moves to the head of the two yielding lines. In reverse, the upper yielding line descends and moves between the two firm lines. We have here a wonderful expression for artistic possibilities. But I want to pursue this still further. In accordance with the two trigrams, art can be divided: song, and image

[e] These three lectures were given at the Goethehaus in Frankfurt.

endowed with form. The internal trigram is song, the external, image endowed with form. Song originates in primarily spiritual tendencies: we are blissful; when we thrust our hands into the Euphrates, the temporal, or liquid element forms song. Fluctuating motion and temporal fantasy are somehow fashioned by receiving content around which they crystallize. Therefore, the Receptive now enters the center, creating clarity in the fluctuation of the temporal process. Clarity then becomes light, because now an object is present to which light can adhere. The trigram Li is the adhering and the sheen, a sheen because it adheres to bodies. Even Mephistopheles was forced to acknowledge that light existed only because of the bodies it adheres to, because of which its beauty unfolds.

Thus light adhering to bodies is the symbol of one part of artistic activity, that of Clarity, Light, the sheen. Another part is the symbol of the form-endowing, the possibility of form-holding, or the spatial that must be controlled by the spiritual. This part is represented by the Resting, for the mountain Ken is a resting trigram. A moment in the tide of time was captured in this hexagram and was surrounded by fashioned form. This belongs to the image.

However, the content-form relationship should not be hypostasized. To be sure, content without form and form without content do not exist. But they have different sources: content in the bosom (soul), and form in spirit; song and image endowed with form are differentiated according to their point of departure.

Obviously, therefore, the nature of this hexagram demonstrates the Chinese concept of the spirit of art.

However, in order to understand this fully we must

consider a twofold development. First, let us consider the nuclear trigrams. These trigrams are seen when the two outer lines of the hexagram are discarded.

upper nuclear trigram   lower nuclear trigram

By discarding the bottom line, the trigram K'an, Water, Abyss, is formed. By discarding the upper line the trigram Chen, the Arousing, appears; two yielding lines above and one firm line below. K'an, Water and Abyss, and Chen, Thunder and the Arousing—these are the hidden nuclear trigrams, and because they are embraced by two strong lines—one above and one below—the work of art is invested with tension and rhythm. Internal tension, produced by the descending Abyss and the ascending Arousing, reveals the internal structure of the art work, a structure produced by the union of spiritual and soul elements.

In addition, the commentary by Confucius states that in the hexagram lie hidden the lines of Heaven and the lines of man.

But before discussing this I would like to mention one other problem contained in the hexagram; namely the problem of line and content. Now here we have a difficult question, because line and substance to the Chinese have connotations different from those of form and content to us, even though, in some instances, their meanings come close. We must not consider a line[2] as a theoretical principle or something formative but, as would the Chinese, it has the potentiality of being formed; it is that which may serve as ornament and embellishment. The line is ready to assume shape, but playfully constantly forms and reforms. However, precisely because of the line's potential, readiness, and need to give shape, it is playful and accomplishes nothing of enduring value in the eternal flux. On the other hand, that which the Chinese call "substance" is not what we consider as substance. Substance is not material. Substance that is to be shaped is Tao. Tao is other-worldly; it exists beyond the phenomenal world. And being other-worldly it cannot enter the phenomenon.

Were we to inquire into the relative importance of line or content, we would be inclined to say in Europe that for a work of art, form is decisive. A work of art, at most, derives stimulation from substance, and only substance that has assumed form can become a work of art. However, if, to the contrary, a line is understood according to my definition, then obviously Tao constitutes the essence of an art work. Tao, however, is not an attribute of an idea or a program. No one has scorned the attribution of a program to his works more than Goethe. No one suffered more than he did when asked what the leading thought of "Faust" might be. Tao here should be understood quite differently. Not an external thought, inserted as leading motif from the outside, but the life principle, the energy that infuses the line with real meaning, causing form to have order so that everything will be in its proper place.

From this point of view, we can understand Confucius' dictum that substance is more essential than line, as well as his other statement that in painting simplicity is the height of perfection.[3] Simplicity foregoes all embellishment, foregoes everything playful, so that form serves only to express the Tao of the work of art. This, Confucius says, is in painting the greatest perfection. But not only in painting; according to the Chinese concept it is true of all art. A similar sentiment is expressed elsewhere: "Emphasizing substance instead of the line [*wen*] is uncouth." A man who does this is not yet cultured. To be sure, he may become cultured, but right now he is "not yet." "He who emphasizes the line [*wen*] instead of substance is a recorder,"[4] or, as we would say, such a person is civilized. He passed through a cultural stage, but culture became mechanized and dead. Only where form and content, line and meaning penetrate each other and result in absolute representation, only there is a cultural flowering, and only there is the highest perfection of art.

This idea is clearly expressed in the two partial trigrams. The upper trigram Ken talks about the "line," the beauty of form, the potentiality of being formed, or perhaps I should say the playful and decorative in multiplicity. The two lower lines are ornamental lines, but precisely therefore they are controlled by the top line, which gives meaning. The solution of the problem then is: spirit, Tao, advances to the top and forms a crystallization line, in accordance with which the elements of form can separate out and organize anew. On the other hand, the lower trigram shows Tao, the meaning, at the bottom. But this does not mean that Tao is embellished by the decorative. Indeed, this would be a wrong interpretation. Rather, here, too, spirit, energy, life, or that which gives shape, is primary and essential. However, that which assumes shape becomes central and provides, as we have seen, the stimulus for light to become visible, so that spirit condenses matter.

The dissimilar relationship of the two elements shows the difference between the two art types. The trigram Ken, the mountain, keeps still, but is also the serene, luminous, clear beauty illuminated from below. It represents plastic art, the art that keeps still as viewed through the eye of the artist. Below is the eye. The image is that of the mountain illuminated and beautified by the fire below. In contrast, song requires the psychic, the eye, which is at once inner light, both mobile and clinging, and which is now shaped, "rounded," and concentrated by means of the spiritual aspect of Tao. Hence, the hexagram illustrates the poem "Song and Image Endowed with Form" from Goethe's *The West-Eastern Divan.*

Although we have so far looked fairly closely at what the spirit of art in China means, I must not fail to indicate briefly two things. One is that we now should be able to see Heaven and man, cosmos and individual joined in a relationship. We should see that macrocosm and microcosm are, as it were, only far-flung parts of one unified energy center. Hence it is written: "The firm and the yielding unite alternately and construct forms." This is the form of Heaven. Beauty or the form of Heaven exists because the firm and the yielding alternate. The firm and the yielding in alternation are the result of the successive steps that the individual parts of the hexagram undergo. Below is the trigram Li, the sun. The sun is the principle of energy, light, the firm. This is one factor of Heaven's form and beauty. Next is the nuclear trigram K'an, the moon, with its yielding line below, a firm central line, and upper yielding line. The moon is feminine, the yielding and is the opposite of the sun. Sun and moon, T'ai Yang and T'ai Yin, the great yang and the great yin, are the pair of opposites that give rise to the forms of Heaven. Here too, the sun is preponderant, the sun being forever luminous, forever strong. The moon is in a state of dependency, gaining light and losing light, being dependent on the sun's supply of light. Above is the upper nuclear tri-gram Chen, the Arousing. Chen signifies the stars, the planets moving about in Heaven. And finally there is the upper trigram Ken, Keeping Still, which is the symbol of the North Star, and which remains fixed in place while all other stars circle about him, as their final pole. Thus manifested in Heaven are day, month, year, and great year—the eon—as the rhythms according to which life develops and which shape events in life. The form and the beauty of Heaven is contained in the celestial bodies.

Still, the firm and the yielding do not form alternately in Heaven alone. These same principles are active on man also. According to the text: "Having form clear and still: this is the form of man." Having form means having shape and having Tao: being shaped in accordance with Tao. Clarity—the lower trigram Li—and stillness—the upper trigram Ken—this is the form of man. Where form, beauty, and art prevail, there is stillness in the battle of existence, a truce that has form, is clear and still. Through this truce all is at peace, and the inner eye perceives things in purity and eternally adorned, and, therefore, considers everything that is as beautiful. At this point, the spectator has withdrawn from the whirlpool of events, has ceased to be driven about by pain and lust, and now stands upon the "Eternal law according to which the rose and lily bloom."[5]

Here, then, is the nucleus of art in man's nature; reposefully observing and permitting the inner light to fall on a world seen in its eternal form will illuminate the world so that it becomes beautiful.

And these are the effects: "If the form of Heaven is contemplated, the changes of time can be discovered. If the forms of men are contemplated, one can shape the world."

It is the assumption here that the world moves and that all existence is perpetually fluid. But flux should be shaped with rhythm, and the forms of Heaven must be observed in order to shape the changes of time. Only then will one recognize the right time for action, for if one's deeds are adapted to the times of Heaven, they will also be confirmed by the times of Heaven. All things being done at their proper time is the harmony of artistic activity. We thus obtain a formative art, art not merely expressed in outward form, but deeply penetrating art shaping the soul according to the "law according to which the rose and lily bloom."

The form of man as beautiful appearance is of tremendous importance. Goethe's *The Fairytale* tells of three world rulers, Wisdom, Appearance, and Force, whose kingdoms persist for long periods of time or forever. In the fairy tale, the Silver King, Appearance, is significant. But only when he appears in purity, undiluted by other energies, when he disclaims everything else except appearance, when he does not pretend to be anything else but what he is, and dismisses all foreign matter from within himself, only then is he a power that molds men. Confucius said that the world can be shaped by Appearance, for the world is most easily shaped through beauty. Such beauty is not pushing or driving from without; it neither forces nor oppresses. Such beauty is effective by means of an inner attraction; such beauty tempts, and moving ahead, is so lovely that all follow with pleasure.

However, having reached this point, limits are imposed on art. Delusion finds peace in art—as we have seen, though, with no finality. There are resting points in the world's motion. Therefore, a curious judgment is appended to this hexagram: "Grace has success. In small matters it is favorable to undertake something," and the image is, "Fire at the foot of the mountain: the image of Grace. Thus does the superior man proceed when clearing up current affairs. But he dare not decide controversial issues in this way." This means: it will not do to decide the final battle according to this axiom. In the controversy of life, art provides rest, recuperation, but not permanent release. The fire at the foot of the mountain blazes and the whole mountain is beautiful. But fire is consumed by the blaze, and the time will come when night will once more submerge everything, and the daily battle will make its claims. The will is silent at the very moment the work of art is born, when the Receptive unites with the creative-formative. However, in accordance with its own law, art exists within the world of change. To be sure, art stands close to the center, but it is nevertheless a product of appearance. All art is appearance, and is dependent on appearance. The energies that shape the work of art originate in the beyond. The work of art, however, like all life, like all things corporeal that appear in time, originates this side of the polar opposites, in the realm where nothing eternally endures, where all things change and are in flux.

Thus at the end we are warned once more not to overestimate this realm, as holy as it may be. Whereas it is necessary to recognize the extent of its power, we dare not progress farther than is permissible. Only then will this realm be completely luminous and fashioned in transparency.

In addition, there are explanations for the individual lines. These, if divested of their curious images, show how to progress from step to step in art—and I am thinking of art in the sense in which we have discussed it tonight—art as the shaping of the shapable, that which is capable of assuming form, or the playful in nature.

The explanation to the first line is: "He lends grace to his toes, leaves the carriage, and walks." What does this mean? The first line is at the very beginning, therefore, the image of the toes. But it is a firm line, and its possibilities do not correspond to its position. The image is that of the carriage. Now the attribute of art, or grace, consists of discarding all nonessential adornments. It consists of leaving out everything superfluous and of confining art to its appointed place. As Confucius said: if locality, duty, or place make travel improper, then it is all right not to travel. Hence, the first step in executing the beauties of artistic creation is to leave out everything unnecessary. Everything should be discarded which is extraneous, everything playful, which goes beyond the Tao, which is merely ornamental without being necessary.

The explanation to the second line sounds almost humorous: "Lends grace to the beard on his chin." The beard on the chin is an accessory, an unimportant part of outward appearance. Here a yielding line in firm place exaggerates that which gives shape and is willing to assume form, the playful; and, therefore, it emphasizes the unimportant as being important. As a result, pretty appearance is transferred to an area where it might be harmless, but where it also cannot be taken seriously. Pretty appearance is still permissible when it moves in conjunction with something superior. This means, to continue the image, that the beard cannot move by itself, it moves together with the mouth onto which it is grown. Hence the beard has the right to move only when it moves together with the mouth. The meaning here is that accessories, outer appearance, ornament, embellishment, and so on are neither good nor bad. They are rather pretty, but they, and the drive to be playful, have prerogatives only in this relationship of dependence. The playful drive must not independently stray into boundlessness, but, subordinate to meaningfulness, must be governed by meaning. Nothing in itself should be cultivated that is not somehow prepared to subordinate itself to meaning.

Now the point has been reached when the work of art is at the height of perfection. The explanation to the third line: "Graceful and moist. Constant perseverance brings good fortune." Here we meet moist and mellow grace:[6] the central line of the nuclear trigram water, which is also the upper line of the trigram fire. Appearance and water penetrate one another, hence moist and mellow grace. The greatest perfection of art occurs when content and form penetrate one another totally, and when the work of art becomes completely transparent. However, here appears a danger and, therefore, the warning: "Constant perseverance brings good fortune." The trigram water also signifies danger, the abyss. But what danger is there in a perfectly lucid work of art? The danger is—and this danger exists whenever a temporary state is to be molded into an enduring state—that now the downgrade is reached. The sun cannot remain at its zenith; at the meridian it must set. The moon cannot remain in the heaven as full moon; the very moment of its fullness is also the moment of its waning. The same holds true for the state of art. When form and its meaning penetrate each other completely, when the work of art is rendered totally transparent, this is only a transitory state, which will necessarily pass. Its danger can be avoided as long as one perseveres in grasping the essential while permitting the transitory to vanish. "Be as the sun at noon, be as the moon that has just become full," is a frequent exhortation. In both cases we are told that concern for the future should not prevent our appreciation and experiencing of the total beauty of today. But at the same time, we dare not grasp artificially the transitory, exposing ourselves to a danger that is avoidable only through constant perseverance, specifically perseverance in forging ahead. There is a verse at the end of the "Chinese-German Times of the Year and Day": "To appease the longing for the distant for what is to come; be actively engaged in the here and now."[7]

The next line introduces us to higher spheres. Six in the fourth place transforms the artist into the ascetic: "Grace or simplicity? A white horse comes as if on wings. He is not a robber. He will woo at the right time." Here is the point where life is silent for a moment, and now the decision must be made how to continue shaping life. Therefore, the question: embellish? Should life be beautified? Or will simplicity do? A white horse comes as if on wings from Heaven. The white horse is also the sun, the sun hurrying past. A white light is simplicity. But now we realize as if fearfully that the will's silence to life, present in art for a mere moment, could turn into an enduring state. A realization of fear and terror. Reassurance, however, follows immediately: "He is not a robber. He will woo at the right time," meaning that an apparently unbearable and terrible state, unbearable when seen as a possibility from without, will become mild and endurable the moment we consciously accept it.

Six in the fifth place is: "Grace in hills and gardens." Beauty now leaves the human sphere once more for nature. And this was precisely the course of Chinese art. The portrayal of man in art, found in antiquity, led at a very early date to the portrayal of nature's mountains and waters. Such art recognizes the law of Tao, Tao that shapes the world. Thus Tao and law are also found where man, the personal element, the human mask, as it were, is no longer visible. This is the spot where lily and rose bloom, where trees live and rocky mountains gaze heavenward. Indeed, Chinese painting did not turn to landscape accidentally, for this development is intimately connected with the spiritual change wrought in the Chinese soul by Buddhism.

The Dhyana school of meditation (Chinese: Ch'an; Japanese: Zen) is a school of Buddhism. And it was this school which, in fact, created Chinese landscape painting. Ch'an painting discards ever more all trimmings, explanations; talk is abandoned for the great silence. Nothingness endows everything that is with form. Thus landscape in Chinese art emerges as the final turn to simplicity, as "Grace in hills and gardens."

The last line is: "Simple grace, no blame." Simple grace means grace without external pretense. This, too, we find in China: highest spirituality is connected with complete absence of outward pretense. A song of antiquity, for example, praises the princess who journeys to her wedding dressed in colorfully embroidered gowns and a simple coat, whereas the coat of her servant who accompanies her to the new home is far more magnificent. Hidden splendor, invisible beauty, suggestiveness as possibility; as potentiality, these are valued most in Chinese art. These however, are also hardest to understand. The Chinese poet T'ao Yüan-ming had a zither without strings. He passed his hand over it and said: "Only a zither without strings can express final stirrings of the heart."[8] For Chinese zither playing is valued most as the expression of the soul, when tones that have ceased to be tones are played. After the note has been struck, the finger glides back and forth over the strings and creates vibrations, but the natural ear does not hear these. Among friends, one tells the other his heart's feelings in these unheard vibrations. Lines and directions, the coordination of shapes in art, there they return from the visible into the invisible sphere. And at the point of their disappearance, where everything transitory is symbol alone, where that which is insufficient (i.e., unreachable) becomes event,[9] there Chinese art enters the eternal, the Heavenly realm.

The hexagram reveals what Chinese thought and felt about the spirit of art. But even though this hexagram is exceedingly important, it is not conclusive. Hence we understand why Confucius sighed at a difficult moment of his life, when he drew this hexagram, and said: "What is grace to me?" Confucius wanted more than final harmony of appearance. He wanted wisdom, creativity, and realism; reshapable realism that can be created with life's energies. And while the hexagram shows the way to reach this goal, it does not exhaust all possibilities.

Now that we have looked at plastic arts and the arts of free fantasy, we see that although no final pronouncements are made, these arts nonetheless hold before us a mirror of eternal energies. They can teach us to transform seeing into contemplation, thereby enabling us to view the world around in eternal ornament. At least then we might find in the battle of life isolated points of rest, where freedom is feasible, a freedom that may lead onward to things more profound.

THE SPIRIT OF MUSIC

Tonight, in our discussion concerning the spirit of music, we shall not speak much about scales and melodies. Rather, we will try to find the origin of music in man's nature and determine its effects on human nature.

There is a saying in China that the nature of man is found there, in the center, where emotions are not yet manifest. In this center is the potentiality of everything to come, but its realization is still distant. Only thereafter emotions appear in their full multiplicity and contrariness. Joy and sorrow, mourning and concern, love, hate, fear, everything appears. Each has a specific direction and attempts to gather all of the latent energies and to accumulate them about itself. The total effect causes man to be carried away by his emotions. Here, therefore, begins the task of music.

The art of music restrains and harmonizes emotions so that they hold one another in check, thus providing the possibility for the center to enlarge into a circle revolving about itself. This is the meaning of the words: "Effect central harmony." Centrality indicates the potentiality of emotions, while harmony is that which causes them to be in accord.

In the *Book of Changes* the spirit of music is represented by the hexagram Yü, Enthusiasm, ☷☳. Yü is composed of the trigram K'un, the Receptive, below; and Chen, the Arousing, above. K'un and Chen combined give the image of Enthusiasm, by Chen, Thunder, resounding from the Earth, K'un.

And this means, when transferred to the stirrings of emotions, that this hexagram is not calmly contemplative, but is internally aroused. An instigating, arousing spark from the unconscious becomes conscious by means of emotions. Among all vague possibilities, emotions establish something; for when I suffer, hate, fear, and mourn, or rejoice, I fix a point for crystallizing the feeling of self, and later for self-consciousness. But this is not a resting point. It emerges from the sea and disappears again. The point is in constant motion, bringing once joy, once sorrow. Therefore, the arousing as such is important. The gates of joy and sorrow are close to one another, and man has only few means for expressing great emotions. A strong emotion provokes tears, both in highest joy and deepest sorrow. What matters is the agitation, the shock of the unconscious which is related to the emergence of consciousness when this shock is inflamed by emotions.

According to the text, "God comes forth in the sign of the Arousing." Emotions cause consciousness in man. But emotions now provoke something that acts over and above the individual human being. Emotions are not mute, they are expressed in sound. The shriek, something like the body of emotions, transcends the individual and creates within other persons the emotion from whom it originated. Thunder resounding from earth is, therefore, a symbol of an emotion that is expressed by the shriek as it resounds from the unconscious.

Thus the barriers that separate man from man are broken down. Although we might assume the group soul to have existed earlier than the individual soul, these group souls—which may have included a number of people—were, however, more strictly divorced from other group souls. And also in this place, Enthusiasm, the Arousing resounding from Earth, is the symbol of breakthrough; dividing barriers between groups give way and men are united in a mutuality of emotion. It is only a step from the shriek to music: the shriek is the material that forms music, just as emotions form the temporal body of the soul.

But on the other hand, it cannot be denied that here lies a certain danger. We are dealing with something completely irrational. There is no logic to the Arousing. To be sure, emotions have causes, but emotions are not reasonable, they somehow never correspond to their causes. Rather their causes ignite latent energies that are later expressed explosively in emotions. Because of this man is, as it were, torn from himself.

The nuclear trigrams indicate this in still other ways. ☵

☶	☵
lower nuclear trigram	upper nuclear trigram

The lower nuclear trigram is Ken, the mountain, Keeping Still; the upper is K'an, water, the Abysmal. The internal structure of the hexagram is, hence, water collected on top of the mountain. There it is restrained, but when water reaches its banks, it rushes without a will of its own headlong into depth and danger, into the abyss. Such is the internal structure of Enthusiasm; an accumulation of emotional energies that break through and then approach the abyss. Birth and death, living and dying approach one another closely here. Chen, the oldest son, first emerges from the mother; in other words, the arousing of emotions is the birth of the soul from the unconscious. At the point, however, when consciousness, the soul, is detached from the unconscious, is the danger of violent shock. Each birth is at once a death, and each birth must, for the new to come into existence, pass through death. An altogether new form of existence must come into being for life to exist in a new set of circumstances. And so it is with Enthusiasm, where life and death stand together, closely related as brothers. When emotions are powerfully expressed, they break the barrier of individuality. The individual is swept along, carried by the power of emotions—whither? He does not know.

For this very reason, Enthusiasm also contains the roots of prophecy, of holy madness. What is holy madness? It is the universal emotion that pulls the individual down into cosmic depths, where life and death are contained, one in the other. This is the Dionysian element that may go as far as butchering life—blood must flow; K'an is also the trigram of blood—so that life can be expressed in its excesses. Perspectives are here disclosed of Shivaite agitations that apportion life and death and that inevitably destroy the individual when cosmic content enters the personality. These are indeed high and great moments, as the individual rises to encompass humanity. The barriers of personality fall, joy and sorrow of humanity accumulate within one's own self, the individual, as it were, pours himself into the collectivity, and unreservedly experiences whatever is allotted humanity.

When the cosmic element thus breaks into the personality and expands it, there are, of course, also dangers. The question now is: where is the root of the movement to which one has given oneself, and to which one has surrendered? And so the point is to find the real utmost depth, where the last central movement in the meaning of world-happening originates. Each premature surrender to individual directions of the movement would by necessity lead to a destruction of individuality, and would necessarily end in catastrophe. There are, as it were, movements in process that pull us along. A powerful personality often sweeps others along, but as such persons are unequal to the soaring flight of this personality, they are dashed to pieces; even as Gretchen was shattered by Faust's personality.

But, on the other hand, expressed emotion is the only means for uniting men. All of the individual's imageries or thoughts are conditioned by his position in human society. Every individual occupies a different position and has a different environment, and even the structure of his receptive organs can cause each man to form an altogether special and individually different world. About this world agreement with others is difficult to reach. Here are final barriers. The individual is mute, because matters about which one can communicate are always discarded remnants of previous powers. That which is most essential in this world cannot be related, precisely because it is impossible to build bridges from one person's inside to another's, or from one experience to the other. Conditions differ too much. But there is one unifying factor. Something vibrates in the primal sound of emotions, a spark jumps from one to the other. And matters impossible to consider in reasonable reflection, or impossible to communicate in a logical manner, become so unconditionally and immediately when a strongly aroused emotion jumps from man to man and gathers them together. This is also surrender (devotion) to movement. Just as an instrument vibrates in conjunction with an equally tuned instrument, the human being too, vibrates in accordance with that which transcends individual separation. This is something primordial, and when touched by the expressive vibrations of a similarly atuned being, it is at once the mainspring and the rallying point of actual life energies.

In proceeding from here to what is told of the effects of music even in Chinese antiquity, we must understand that it is an attempt to express a remarkable experience; vibration in unison by two human beings will cause communication. A story is told of two friends. One was playing the zither and the other said: "I hear mighty waters roar, I see mountains pile up high." The friend felt as if he were standing at the great mountain, T'ai-shan, while waterfalls were gushing down.[10] The ability to communicate an emotion is this great; it fills the tones themselves so that even a part of the emotion's cause was carried over and reproduced visually. Still, certain limitations are present here, and in China these limitations are also recognized. There is a charming little story about Confucius. Once his favorite disciple heard him play, and becoming fearful, he said: "The master has thoughts of murder." This happened while Confucius watched a spider weave its web around a fly, and thus expressed what he saw in the movement of the chords. The disciple's ability to be moved by the master's playing was so great that he understood the emotion; but he failed to understand its cause and merely noted that thoughts of murder were involved. He was unable to determine whether these thoughts concerned the murder of man or fly. Though he recognized the direction, he failed to see the dynamics of the master's music.

Confucius himself is an example of how far the spirit of music might compel surrender to the Arousing. Once, while with a famous music master, he heard a melody. First he learned its tones, then its spirit, later the heart, emotions, significance, and the thoughts of the man who had invented this music. Although the music master was already satisfied with Confucius' playing of the melody, he still could not desist. Only when a vision of a dark, tall shape confronted him, did he say: "I see him, of dark, tall shape; exalted being, a creator among men." Then the music master bowed before Confucius and said: "Indeed, this melody derives from King Wen, the creator of our culture."[11] The extent of potential communication among men can thus be seen. It is clearly also important that we surrender, not only to a peripheral movement, but that the movement be in the very center of our nature. To be sure, it is possible to swim in every stream for some time, but the direction of our innermost nature must be grounded there where the cosmic essence has its source.

It is even more important that leaders of mankind recognize how to apply Enthusiasm, rather than be drawn along by its stimulating energies. And here is once more a secret of great music. According to the text: "Devotion to movement: this is Enthusiasm. Because Enthusiasm shows devotion to movement, heaven and earth are at its side. How much the more then is it possible to install helpers and set armies marching! Heaven and earth move with devotion, therefore sun and moon do not swerve from their courses, and the four seasons do not err. The holy man moves with devotion; therefore fines and punishments become just, and the people obey. Great indeed is the meaning of the time of Enthusiasm."

Surrender (devotion) to movement, according to the text, is a means of governing, of creating order among separated and isolated individuals. It is the means of lawful and meaningful unification of society, even in the most dangerous situations. Helpers are installed, armies are set marching—these are the examples. Here, too, is a connection with the spirit of music. On the one hand, music as a great art unites men in common joy, and the power of sound creates harmony when the force of darker emotions awakens. On the other hand, however, music is the energy that kindles the courage to face death; the singular energy that can set armies marching, and enables men to fight last battles.

The potentiality of music, active in Enthusiasm, is thus obvious. But only when the leader himself surrenders to the Arousing can he apply these potentialities. The man who wholly surrenders to its movement, who is moved by the stirrings of the soul, the soul of the group, or the soul of the collectivity, only such a man is destined to be a leader of men. Only he who feels with, and is enthusiastic with all mankind, is made to be a leader of others. Therefore, surrender to movement that must be stimulated in others must first be experienced by the leader. Only the experienced emotion can be transferred to others. This is the meaning of the interesting sentence that even Heaven and Earth are devoted to movement. Nor do Heaven and Earth know restraints. In Heaven the constellations move along their paths, nowhere a hand to hold them, nowhere a rope to bind them. They are free—this means they are completely devoted to movement—such is the

Chinese concept of freedom. The constellations move along freely, and being completely free they are unrestrained, and therefore their primary sense can be effective. Therefore, neither sun nor moon yields from its established course. Similarly, Earth does not seek to retain anything. When spring comes, the Earth receives spring; when spring leaves, the Earth permits spring to depart and prepares for the summer. And for this reason the seasons do not err. Devotion to movement is the secret of regular temporal activity. Therefore, it is imperative to release to freedom that point in human nature where Tao is dormant. As a result, freedom for others is created and activated. Tao, Law of the world, is given shape.

If properly understood, this is something that bestows the greatest power on earth. There are different types of leaders; there are, as it were, different degrees of devotion to movement. Each time, surrender to movement produces leadership qualities, but the depth of the movement's origin determines the durability and power of a leader. A person who surrenders to the moods of the day, who gives voice to the dissatisfaction of the masses, momentarily becomes leader of the masses. For one moment he is the man in whom the people recognize themselves. Such a person's sense of timing causes him to select the significant moment in the course of events, and he becomes the great man of the hour. As he rides the crest of the wave he appears great to the whole world. But such surrender to a superficial movement of waves moved by the wind necessarily results in the descent that follows the ascent. The more on the surface a movement within a person is, and the more it is intended to draw the masses, the sooner it ends. A true ruler alone recognizes, in spite of opposition, the will of the nation—or better, the will of "nationhood" [*Volkheit*]. He who is devoted to seeing not only individuals, to knowing not merely the changing opinions of the day, but to knowing what nationhood desires, is a ruler whose movements are effective in devotion.

Therefore, for example, the secret of Confucius' success is discovered. In recent times his significance has been questioned; it has been said that he had little originality. But in fact, Confucius was and is effective because he had a penetrating recognition of the will of mankind—the will of mankind which is the voice of the Divinity—and, therefore, he at first acted in a way that was apt to conceal the results of his actions. Long after the surface movements of his time had calmed down, it became increasingly clear that what he had done and what he had wanted was a stimulus that acted on generations to come.

The course of the spirit of music is expressed in the following pronouncement on the image: "Thunder comes resounding out of the earth: the image of Enthusiasm. Thus the ancient kings made music in order to honor merit, and offered it with splendor to the Supreme Deity, inviting their ancestors to be present." An image unfolds of Earth, Heaven, and ultimate metaphysical energies, all connected through the spirit of music. Merit is honored with music, expressed in tone and gesture. For tone and gesture in ancient China are brother and sister, they are simultaneous expressions of a deep emotional power. Whatsoever lives in the heart is expressed in sound, and growing in intensity, is expressed by movement, so that each tone and each movement are the expression of internal animation. And this brings us to the holy dramatic performances where musical sounds and the dancers' symbolic movements represented cosmic events: the dance of the stars. Here we touch on excitement, which apprehends the law of cosmic aspects. Represented is the Tao of the world and, therefore, the world's mysteries. Everyone who experiences these is pulled deeply toward the direction of eternity.

Merits are honored in this way. All cultural achievements are honored with this music and are offered the Supreme Lord; the Lord in Heaven who lets the stars move in their courses. And ancestors of ages past, masters who once were creative, are invited to congregate about the Supreme Deity. The Supreme Deity, born of the spirit of music as the concept of man, is in China not an abstract idea. Just as there is a Heaven, there is a deity. But this unity contains multiplicity. Contained in unity is an infinite multitude of ancestors and ghosts, of energies and powers. The stream of emotions, the harmony of music expressed in holy pantomimes is also the spirit that permeates the Supreme Deity. Man comes in contact with God through the spirit of music.

Let us take still one more step. Emotions are mobile, they can be aroused, and they can be intensified to ecstasy, as all prophecy is somehow ecstasy and holy madness. Emotions, however, are subject to other laws. They are like the waves of the sea; when lashed into fury they rise and then sink once more. Emotions are subject to a sequence that obeys fixed laws, and not even the strongest emotion endures. Hence, if the spirit of music is to create something of enduring value, one further step is necessary. This in turn is expressed in the hexagram Ts'ui, ☷☱, Gathering Together.

Ts'ui differs from Yü by having one additional firm

line. A gathering together, massing, is necessary for movement, or the emotion of surrender, not to evaporate into empty air. Something enduring must emerge. And toward this end, it is absolutely necessary to form a focal point. The firm, fifth line of Ts'ui is the symbol of man, the representative of movement. For energy to be effective in some way, it must be represented by a personality. Movement on earth requires a leader, a personality, in order to become an enduring movement. The hero, the king, the great man, or whatever else he may be called in the *Book of Changes*, is such a personality; in regard to this hexagram, where we are dealing with truly great relationships, it is the king. "Gathering Together. Success. The king approaches his temple. It furthers one to see the great man. This brings success. Perseverance furthers. To bring great offerings creates good fortune. It furthers one to undertake something." Emotions become action.

Music is transferred to religion, because the great man who approaches the temple, the great man whom it furthers to see, is the religious hero; molder and creator of humankind. From time to time such a man appears, appropriating to himself and molding, according to his image, larger and smaller areas, by allowing his body to be eaten and his blood to be drunk. Here emerges the esoteric aspect of sacrifice. "To bring great offerings creates good fortune." In barbaric times the king, in whom God manifested himself, who was man and god or the son of god, was immolated at the height of ecstasy. He was the sacrifice for his kin, and his overflowing blood expiated those who belonged to him. Chinese culture long ago transformed this into symbol. The representative of the Creative must somehow sacrifice himself, and his spiritually flowing blood is used to nourish those who belong to his community. Here, then, music terminates in religion. The two are intimately related, and religion in a way elucidates the content of music. Logos descends from his heights, and sound—the shriek—is joined by myth. Myth unites men within the symbol, it embraces men, and they are far more moved than they would have been by mere sound, for myth is the music of symbolism. Therefore, it is also clear that myth is fulfillment. In myth, the dark substratum—sacrifice, final renunciation and final giving—which makes union possible, is interpreted in a way as to indicate luminous heights. The hexagram Gathering Together has the Joyous above and the Receptive or devotion below. Devotion to joyousness, devotion to the greatest joy in man; and hence the deepest meaning of music terminates in ultimate religiousness.

But even here, harmony is the core of the spirit of Eastern wisdom. To be sure, the deep origin of Western tragedy is not foreign to Eastern wisdom either, but these depths are for it only partial, and not final in themselves. Height and depth are united by Logos, by Tao. Joyousness, and surrender to joyousness as the final redemption of myth, supply the energy necessary for order among men. Surrender to joyousness forms and shapes men; force neither of arms nor of law, but joyousness alone makes it easy for men to follow. Joyousness is garbed in beauty, showing itself pleasantly to men, so that from within they are compelled to submit easily and willingly to its regulations. Ultimately, this is the greatest idea that came to life in China as the spirit of music and as the spirit of religion.

THE SPIRIT OF THE ART OF LIVING

We now have reached the last possible aspect that art can mean. This is the order of change, the art of action, in short, the art of living.

As the first hexagram we have Lü, Treading [Conduct], no. 10, ☰☱. Treading has a twofold sense: as stepping on something, and as behavior in accordance with proper conduct.[12] Therefore, the *Book of Changes* uses Lü to stand for Li, proper conduct. Hence the concern here is with the art of action by means of proper conduct.

Lü is composed of the trigrams Tui, the Joyous, below, and Ch'ien, the Creative, above. The lake below, Heaven above; the youngest daughter below, the father above. Among the eight trigrams, they are the first and the last, respectively. The Creative is most distinguished; all other trigrams are somehow directly or indirectly derived from it. The youngest daughter, the trigram Tui, is the farthest removed, or last derived. The unequivocal distance between the two removes all doubts, and produces order.

The character of the two trigrams is joy and strength, or firmness. These two attributes produce proper conduct and, therefore, part of the appended judgment reads: "Treading shows the basis of character. It is harmonious and attains its goal. It brings about harmonious conduct." Harmonious conduct is possible because the two trigrams are moving in the same direction. Both ascend, one following the other. Their harmony however, is neither simple nor self-evident. Both trigrams have their special place in Heaven; Tui is in the west and is mid-autumn; Ch'ien is in the northwest, and indicates the ninth month, when autumn enters winter. Tui is the time of harvest. In the west, in Heaven, it has the quadrant of the white tiger. The white tiger is a terrible, death-dealing element, as, indeed, white is the color of mourning. The element of both trigrams is metal, the weapon, indicating the judgment that lies in autumnal air. Thus a person, desirous of learning conduct, or the art of living, perceives a monstrous, demoniacal, overpowering element—a threatening danger that deprives him of power. This inward pressing aspect of the divinity, the numen, should always be feared, because it is something that confronts a person with overwhelming power.

And this divine power (numen) which also represents destiny, leaves us no choice. It stands before us inescapably and demands that we come to terms with it. Destiny is not easy, simple, or playful; we have a condition of utmost seriousness. Here the Creative, as indicated by the upper trigram Ch'ien, the judging, demands an account. The year has come to an end, autumn is past, now we will see what can survive and what must perish. Now is the time when the fruit of spring is returned once more into the wheel of changing events.

The four seasons turn like a mighty wheel. Life ascends, blossoms, bears fruit, sends its seeds below, and, when the dark half of the year comes, everything is returned again. That which is transitory must disappear irretrievably. As an old saying has it: "Heaven combats the beings in the sign of the Creative." The great fighter, who combats all beings that have emanated from him, and that have entered the world in the sign of the Arousing, stands in the northwest, where the year nears its end. Every individual must go through this battle; the battle of the Creative with the transitory. The combat is, of course, utterly serious. Obviously, the human being will become aware that the enemy is not battling from without and that the combat is not merely a coincidence. Destiny is outside the gate and the threshold must be crossed, even if it is guarded by the brazen guardian, Creative energy, deeply and seriously penetrating energy. We can understand why a person trembles, why he attempts to evade, why he wants to steal by this time of reproachful, severe gravity; or why, in wanton defiance, he would want to disavow it, explain it away in order to resist. But destiny stands still and waits. No mortal can escape it. Every human being who searches for eternity must give an account of himself. Everyone will eventually meet the guardian of the threshold, when the way of holding one's own in the combat will be determined.

Here, too, Goethe found the words. Simply and yet subtly, they convey his greatest wisdom:

> Musst nicht widerstehn dem Schicksal,
> aber musst es auch nicht fliehen;
> wirst du ihm entgegengehn,
> wirds dich freundlich nach sich ziehn.[13]

> You should not resist fate,
> nor need you escape it;
> if you go to meet it,
> it will guide you pleasantly.

This is the interpretation of the hexagram Lü, Treading. The point is to assume the proper attitude and to make the right decision. There is no denying the seriousness of this issue. Should a person attempt to do so, should anyone fancy himself strong enough to explain away the enormity of this task, he would succumb and be destroyed. Because in denying destiny, we deny ourselves. Neither is escape successful. Destiny is not external, but is something creative; and since everything creative is the progenitor of all creatures, the living father who dwells within us, how could one escape? How, indeed, can anyone escape the creative force that is within ourselves and by means of which we exist? Destiny is unavoidably operative.

At this point there is the information: "Will you go to meet him," that is the Treading. The youngest daughter is incapable of battling with this powerful force. Therefore, cheerfully and obediently she follows the father. She follows him even where the path is dangerous and when a decision may mean life or death. Such simplicity and unpretentiousness is faith, if we are to ascribe any significance to this much misunderstood word; faith, derived from reality and always applicable to reality. This kind of faith is love of destiny. Neither love of happiness nor fear of unhappiness, but free of fear and hope, such faith chains humankind's two greatest enemies.[14] This faith is victory, for it knows how to guide creative energy toward the result of progress.

Also this is contained in the hexagram. Treading does not tarry. We are not concerned with a static condition, but with a moment of gravest danger, of far-reaching decisions, a moment as if of razor sharpness. And the moment can be surmounted only if the proper movement, the movement of progress is found. To continue in danger would entail death. For no mortal being can indefinitely tolerate facing the Creative naked and unprotected. We can endure this battling Creative only by advancing each moment.

Here now we see the germinating point of proper

conduct. That which is the final truth for the individual is transferred to all humankind. Once more the secret of proper conduct is differentiation, a differentiation of high and low, which is dynamic. The waters below Heaven come from above, and by coming from above, they have absorbed the energy proper to such movement. Therefore, all productive conduct differentiates between high and low as a graded, dynamically active differentiation, in the sense that all relationships are somehow based on levels of high and low, where no temporal relationship has an absolute position. Nothing is absolutely high. Everything high on earth is subject to Heaven. Even the ruler of mankind, the son of Heaven, has a subordinate position to the father, the great ancestor. Similarly, there is no absolute depth. A person may be simple and modest, and yet somehow, somewhere a situation exists where a person can give or promote. In this way all mankind is harnessed into a coordinated system, a graded system of a movement from above to below, which is dynamic. Only because of this proper conduct arises.

Proper conduct appears to be uniformity for, after all, proper conduct is what everyone does. But the secret of proper conduct is in inequality. Uniformity alone cannot give rise to proper conduct. To be sure, uniformity might produce rule and regulation or law and force. But tedious force and brutal law never led people to convictions that legitimately resulted in proper conduct (the term includes that which produces proper conduct and proper conduct achieved). Instead, as Confucius said:[15] "Force produces only alienation and people transgress secretly that which is public regulation." Hence, a system of enforced mechanical equality is necessarily ineffective. Only fundamental inequality as a part of man's nature (indeed, there are no two people alike) can give rise to proper conduct as an orderly system of human relationships. And therefore, the image states: "Heaven above, the lake below: the image of Treading. Thus the superior man discriminates between high and low, and thereby fortifies the thinking of the people." Differences in levels are productive, because the low spontaneously are induced to imitate the high. They need not be forced; it is their heart's desire to imitate the superior in everything, and to be equal. Proper conduct begins in this way, and eventually those who lag behind will be attracted by a force that activates from within and does not push from without. Here, once more, we see a universe moved from within, without external manipulation. And since the universe is also within the human being, internal universal order leads to order without by the force of necessary differentiation.

The individual thus confirms his destiny by confirming his mind when he consciously enters and arranges his being in this transcendent relationship. For this is the important point: everyone must find his place. Fundamentally, positions do not differ in relationship to the absolute. Each temporal position is oriented upward and downward, and therefore a person in any particular position need not know his place on the scale. It is, however, important that an appropriate position be assumed. The trigram Tui is below, trigram Ch'ien is above. Each one in its appropriate place. And precisely because the trigrams stand in their proper places—what must be above, is above, and what must be below, is below—precisely because of this, it is possible to be satisfied with one's destiny. In the entire hexagram we find one single weak line that is surrounded by five strong lines. This weak line is the point of transition where nature enters man. (The two lower lines are the Earth, the central lines are man, the two upper lines, Heaven.) This line, by standing in the place of transition and advancing, therefore, controls forces that press in from all sides. Here begins the vision of man in the universe. The human being is the weakest of all creatures, for nature gave him neither laniary teeth, nor horns; neither claws nor armor plating. Helplessly and defenselessly he is born into a world of monsters, helplessly he lies there, more helpless than any other creature on earth. No other creature except man is that unfit, is that dependent on the world; on external kindness. After several days or weeks, all animals are able to live in their environment, with the means at their disposal; but human beings require years, decades, before they are independent.

This weak creature is now put in an environment full of dangers, full of all kinds of strong forces. But still the tiger does not bite the man. The judgment says, "Treading upon the tail of the tiger. It does not bite the man. Success." This is based on the yearly image, because the great tiger on Heaven is the representative of cosmic, overpowering forces. Now man must advance and tread on the tail of the tiger. The trigram Ch'ien is in front, trigram Tui follows. But in spite of this great daring, which is the point here, the tiger does not bite the man. Is it because of his helplessness, this helpless joy, which after all is the greatest power on earth? The smiling eyes of a child are more powerful than any malice, any anger. Such eyes disarm even the most depraved, and the tiger does not bite the man who knows to approach him in this way. This then is the art of action. It presupposes being childlike in its highest sense, it presupposes that the joy of the heart, internal joy, is preserved intact, and inner trust is offered to one and all. Such trust is accompanied by dignity. The hexagram Treading has Tui, Joyousness, within, and Ch'ien, Strength, without. In some way the image is reminiscent of the boy in the *Novelle*,[16] who tames the lion with joy and therefore represents a person confronted by cosmic energies. And this constitutes the secret of proper conduct, conduct as the art of living.

Now we have art at its height, art on an individual basis; that is the harmonious integration of the personality into its fate-relationships. Fate-relationships are given, but it is freedom that allows us to acknowledge them. As a result we can confront the relationships harmoniously so that conduct will change into progress.

Still another aspect must be considered. How are we to pass on our experience, the accumulated wisdom, energy, belief, or ways of adapting? As human beings we are not put in this world to enjoy ourselves only, or always to accept things; each acceptance also involves the duty to pass it on. Indeed, the true meaning of the world is that generation after generation emerges from a great and mysterious depth, and each generation is entrusted by the preceding one with the sacred heritage. Each generation must enrich it and pass it on. And only by passing on the enriched heritage, creative energies keep flowing. Therefore, we must face this serious question in its totality as well as in its details: how is the great heritage, which we have recognized as our highest good, to be passed on? How are we to preserve continuity, for we dare not stand at the end of a chain. Nothing terrifies us more than to be last in a line, and it is most terrifying when irretrievable singular, spiritual goods are involved, or when we cannot judge consequences. Especially today we must face the grave danger, the last question asked of art: are we able to rescue the spiritual heritage from the vulgarity pressing in on us from all sides? Art that succeeds to solve even this problem of humankind is good art. Such art passes on spirit and flame kindled in the heart, and it will continue to kindle, propagate, and guard the sacred fire, so that it may continue to burn.

All of us are concerned with this problem. And in every act, in every place where we confront such seriousness, we also confront the question: how will it be possible to do this? The *Book of Changes* gives its answer in a beautiful way. In the hexagram discussed above, the yielding line is in the third place. And by changing the next, the other human line also into a yielding line, we obtain the hexagram Chung Fu, Inner Truth, no. 61, ☲☱.

Now there are two firm lines above and below, without and within, and in the center are two yielding lines. Not only is the hexagram deeply significant, the two Chinese words, *chung fu*, also have a peculiarly imaginative strength. The character *fu* is simply a bird's claw with the offspring, or egg, underneath. It has, therefore, the connotation both of hatching and of transferring life to a germinating enclosure. *Chung*, the middle, means that the central process of hatching, the central energy of animation, contained in truth or in trustworthiness, is active. This hexagram is the energy of inner truth, truth understood here in its deepest meaning, truth as harmony with Heaven.

We further discover that this hexagram has other strange aspects. It very obviously consists of the doubled trigram of light. The trigram light has a weak line in the middle and a strong line above and below. Chung Fu has two weak lines in the middle, and two strong lines above and below. It is, therefore, like an enormously projected light. Within, however, as latent opposition, is the great darkness; that is fire that originates in the water of the abyss has released the light without harming it. And, therefore, light now has power even over the creatures of darkness. Such is the meaning of the strange words: "Inner Truth. Pigs and fishes. Good fortune. It furthers one to cross the great water. Perseverance furthers." The representatives of the dark powers of water are pigs and fishes, the least spiritual of all animals. But the power of light is so great that its transforming influence extends even to fishes and pigs, the mute and unspiritual. It is, indeed, amazing how the hexagram answers almost verbally our justifiable worry of how to preserve the spiritual heritage, when the unspiritual masses, the disjointed masses, threaten its destruction. For this is the answer: through the power of inner truth.

Since this, however, touches on matters occult, I merely want to convey the part handed on to me, and leave it up to the reader to make of it whatever he wishes.

How does inner truth begin? Through a peculiar play in change. Inside the hexagram it is empty, for the two weak lines signify emptiness. Therefore, in the actual center is emptiness, Nothing. If, next, we examine the two partial trigrams—the inner or lower trigram, and the outer or upper trigram—we find in the center of each a strong, heavenly, line, the great One that originates in the Creative. Although this is difficult to reconcile, it must be done. The empirical ego, the ego born of delusion and prejudice, the ego born of the petty purposes that yield new purposes in the very moment of fulfillment, this ego must die. When the ego, as it oscillates hopelessly between cause and effect, between purpose and fulfillment, desirous of pleasure, and languishing in pleasure for desire, when this ego is extinguished, great Silence and Emptiness begins. The noise of the day ceases, and all at once the great unearthly light, the double light, shines forth and as a mystic occurrence, the One is detached and enters man, filling his heart and making it firm. And whenever this One arrives from out of creative depths, contact between man and the universe is established. Such contact in turn unfolds the magical forces, though it is not magic that unfolds them, but Truth. And, according to Confucius, their effects will be felt even in far-away places. Truth, having been realized at this point, can be effective at any other point; wherever proper conditions prevail, where the moment is ripe, and when the time has come. Hence spatial or temporal distances are of no consequence. It is merely necessary to comprehend fully ultimate realities, and to unite with that which has detached from heavenly depths, for this creates further reproductive energies. When internal forces are transformed into Truth, then there is victory; then the masses are powerless, they can do no harm. And our only concern now is to make our heart wholly true, and to make actual contact with what we know to be Truth. Such contact is possible when the empirical self is silent, when it has died so that God can live in us. Ultimate art exists when this Truth is present—the art to shape our destiny and the art that enables us to pass on creatively that which we ourselves have received.

This may sound proud and arrogant, but it is not.

Creation takes place in broad spheres, yet all life, whether great or small, must be passed on creatively to assure its continued existence. Destiny determines the sphere of our activity, the field of our duties. But, it is up to us to perceive these duties from the deepest possible viewpoint and verify them to ourselves. Then their fulfillment is assured.

Constancy in Change

Lass den Anfang mit dem Ende
Sich in Eins zusammenziehn!
Schneller als die Gegenstände
Selber dich vorüberfliehn!
Danke, dass die Gunst der Musen
Unvergängliches verheisst:
Den Gehalt in deinem Busen
Und die Form in deinem Geist.

Be then the beginning found
   With the end in unison,
Swifter than the forms around
   Are themselves now fleeting on!
Thank the merit in thy breast,
   Thank the mould within my heart,
Thank the Muses' favor blest
   Ne'er will perish, ne'er depart.

Goethe[1]

We live today in a critical era. Humankind has experienced much; and I might say that my life, as well as life generally, appears to be suffused with difficulties. Although we should acknowledge this fact, we should not become discouraged. If, indeed, we stand today at the crossroads of two eras, and a number of signs seem to bear this out, it must also be true that times of hardship are inevitable. For mankind can only find the ability to work together, and fashion a new time, when it has reached into the greatest depth and there found contact with reality.

It is customary in China to concentrate one's energies and to prepare for a task even before the task has been confronted. Therefore, according to ancient usage, the course of the year is understood as the coming year with its roots in the old year. A new year begins precisely at the moment when the old year is at its lowest ebb and when the energies of light have almost disappeared. The new year has as yet no reality; it is idea. Still invisible, the new idea descends. Hence it is important to greet the new, invisible idea, even before its appearance, because thereafter one must be prepared to follow developments step by step.

And so it is that constancy in change gives strength for meeting the new time, and for shaping it productively.

Such are the thoughts that are related to three hexagrams in the *Book of Changes*, which represent the different steps of constancy in change.

PATIENCE

The first of these hexagrams is Ching, the Well. The Well here is understood as a common fact of life. It is not something individually isolated, but is a way of appropriating life. The well is at the center of a Chinese settlement; the village is grouped around the well, people come and go to the well, and the fields of the village spread out from this center. Since the fields of ancient China were situated about a central field where the well was found, the location of the well is also the center of work.[2] From this we are led to reflect on how to appropriate life and how to dispense life. Appended to the image is the following: "The Well. The town may be changed, but the well cannot be changed. It neither decreases nor increases. They come and go and draw from the well. If one gets down almost to the water and the rope does not go all the way, or the jug breaks, it brings misfortune."

The idea of the well is formed by wood, ☰, descending and bringing up water, ☵. This is also considered to be the image of organic life. Among the elements, wood is thought of as organically active. Wood, the organic form of existence, gathers inorganic matter in the form of water saturated with nutritive materials, and by bringing these up, uses them for growth. Here is the example of how life begins and grows. And the underlying idea of this concept considers life an inexhaustible spring. On earth we find all kinds of substances, such as minerals, the presence of which we detect by mechanical means. But the mechanical existence of external objects may be considered only one half of the world. In addition to the crystallized part, there is still another, called life.

Life is not a special form of existence, in the sense that we somehow add a life force to other, different mechanical forces of the inorganic world. This would substantiate the doctrine of Vitalism in its assertion that life's energies are added as a plus to other inorganic energies, and it is this addition on which life is dependent. If this were the case, life would be finite, for every addition eventually reaches a point of exhaustion. We would, indeed, have to count on life's eventual cessation; the end that is inevitable for all inorganic existence, even though its energies and mass can be conserved. All inorganic existence, it seems, will meet a condition of involution where, when all forces are equalized, only a general equilibrium remains. Under such circumstances, nothing is cold and nothing is warm; and because of this there is no tension, and a lukewarm death enfolds the world. Were life any of these energies, it would follow these same laws, and all we could expect is to meet a tepid death.

Life, however, is the exact opposite of death, and the energy of life is neither visible nor within matter; life's energy differs essentially from all other forces. Life is diametrically opposed to such forces. The secret of all existence may very well be that in addition to forces active in matter, there is the mystery that these energies are forever redirected so as to bring about something new. Mechanical forces in themselves do not create anything new. Causality conditions their flow and ebb, and strict necessity conditions development. By understanding these energies, one can predict today what is to happen ten thousand years hence. But the unfolding, the folding asunder in time, is only one of the forms of appearance. It is not real, for each effect, each consequence, is contained in the cause.

And now the ring must be broken. But not broken so that at any point its laws would cease to be valid. Indeed, Europe's most important contribution to the knowledge of nature is probably its emphasis on causality, the sequence of cause and effect, and its universal validity. In effect, we have nowhere a point where this relationship could be rejected and where we could say: "This is a miracle. Here is empty space, where somehow something scientifically inaccessible is happening; where something disappears and something new, previously unconditioned, appears." But while causality is valid throughout the world of appearances, we find in this world, and acting through it, something that is not subject to causality. It is not a separate higher or lower world, but is inseparably united with this world, and acts through it. It is valued, knows values, and creates values. This strange interior of the world—if we may designate this relationship so—is inseparably united with the exterior. One could not speak of it as the seed, and of something else as the shell. Nature has neither seed nor shell;[3] both inseparably interpenetrate one another, and yet there is an essential difference. This system of values, which is the basis of all the arts, is present together with the system of causality.

Here is an interesting phenomenon. It seems that a mechanical effect can take two directions in the organism: constructive or destructive. Causality does not give us the reason. For this is a neutral point, the point where causality enters the phenomenon. Whatever lies beyond phenomenon must always be inaccessible to science. However, we see that certain chemicals support and nourish the life of our bodies and maintain them. On the other hand, only a second later, without essential changes in the body's chemical composition, we may find that this same causality, acting in reverse, results in the gradual decomposition and decay of the body. It is the same causality and the same substances; once working this way, and once working that; both activities can be scientifically examined. Indeed, we would be superstitious were we to assume that living organisms are less accessible to science than dead organisms. On the contrary, the opportunity and duty of science is to investigate to an even greater extent the complicated constructional texture customarily designated as life.

Now that we have established that life is not a thing among other things, but that it is life that causes other things to act so as to assume value (rather than being merely causally conditioned), we can once more return to our Chinese image of the well.

Our hypothesis was that life is endlessly abundant. "The town may be changed, but the well cannot be changed. It neither decreases nor increases. They come and go and draw from the well." The history of mankind is one of infinite and continuous changes. These are not only technological changes. To be sure, technology has wrought many far-reaching changes in our lives, and the effects of technology are in turn related to transformations in society. The structure of society has changed as much in the course of history as our external lives have been altered by technology. Ways of associating and social organization are always differently constituted. There was a very specific form of social organization in matriarchal antiquity, whereas an entirely different, though again well-defined, society can be seen in the form of patriarchal culture. Their differences are clearly defined. And moving on in history, we have a still different social organization in feudal society. Still later there is the form of the centralized bureaucratic state, and finally the form of organized economic cooperation. Hence, there is an incredible diversity of forces and ideas that have shaped human society. And I believe that this also constitutes development. As is the case with technology, so here, too, is increasing diversity and progress; progress insofar as social life becomes more prosperous and gratifying. Recurrent reverses that we suffered in the course of history must not mislead us. This is especially true at the present time, when we have been seemingly fooled by the expectations we have brought to the new day of the future. But this is a time of setbacks, which will come more than once. We must not forget that the path leads upward and forward.

However, these social changes—compared here to

a city that stands once in one place, once in another—
should not be mistaken for the ultimate, basic condition of life. For as long as man is constructed into, and
interwoven with, the fabric of nature, he is subject to
certain laws of nature. In this fabric of nature, man is
the point of transition; or perhaps the point where
warp and woof cross. From a spiritual point of view,
man is the mysterious being in whom the Creative of
the world ascends into consciousness. These ultimate
bases of life remain unchanging. And certain laws
connected with them must be followed by all forms of
human society. When such laws are violated, and nature is assaulted, revenge results as the necessary
reaction of illness and death.

Thus the well, life, is an enduring supply and an
unchanging form of existence. Life is as great and inexhaustible as the world. The well does not decrease
and does not increase; people draw from it day in and
day out, and it nourishes them. It is like the water,
which ascends to heaven and descends again as rain.
This rotation of tension and release, of ascent and descent, maintains external life on our planet.

It is the same with the soul. Here also is an inexhaustible supply of life, and here also are tension-
creating forces. That which has been adapted from
the general supply is conveyed into channels of individual existence, and conscious human life is produced. Because of the inherent tension, life surges
upward and descends once more as new supply. The
inexhaustible circulation of life is like the circulation
of water on earth.

We know the energy that causes water to circulate:
it is the sun and her unlimited and divine energy.
Perhaps we ought to assume the existence of a similar
energy for spiritual realms—a sort of central sun.

Goethe called it once "God-nature," because inner necessity maintains the circulation of life in constant motion as a rotation of tension and release. Every release produces a tension similar to the one that caused it. And yet the human being is inclined to stipulate beginning and end. This inclination is caused by the fact that his own life emerges and disappears as a temporary and temporal phenomenon, and he, therefore, projects onto the world whatever is important in his individual existence. Hence, he would reverse the law of causality, emptying, as it were, until a first cause is reached; or he would project causality forward until an end of everything is reached. I believe these questions about the beginning and the end of the world to be idle questions. Such questions transfer causality, applicable to the phenomenal world only, onto a world where there is no more phenomenon, but where phenomenon originates and ends. These are idle endeavors. One may produce fantasies, even scientific fantasies, but not certainties. Regarding this topic we have not progressed further than the philosopher Lieh Tzu's notion, concerning whom there is an interesting story. A man once worried that Heaven and Earth would perish. He neither slept nor ate, until one day a scholar happened by who explained that Heaven is an accumulation of air, and Earth an accumulation of the Firm, and that, therefore, neither Heaven nor Earth can perish. Both were pleased with one another until a third man came and said: "Are you not aware that Heaven and Earth are only material things? Heaven and Earth consist of many individual phenomena which are not dependable, and which must by necessity some day perish." Then Lieh Tzu said: "Whether the world will collapse some day, or endure eternally, is something we cannot know. And the sage does not bother about it."[4] I believe that even today we are no further than this point of view. We may rest assured in the realization that there is neither surplus or deficiency in the stream of life. The well does not decrease, no matter how much one draws from it; but neither will it increase if one seeks to conserve its energies, instead of using them. Life is an inexhaustible spring; it does not decrease and does not increase, and is at everyone's disposal.

But here we are at a point where life ceases to be merely this rich activity of the force of existence. Now personal responsibility begins. It is a fact that life is not everywhere powerful to the same degree, and that lifeless matter is not everywhere equally transparent to the forces of life. We know of inert, heavy, and cumbersome things, and we also know of conditions where the heaviness of gravity is apparently completely discarded, and we see genius at work. And we are forced to consider what causes this vast difference. Is not all matter subject to uniform laws, and is not all life inexhaustibly at our disposal?

The answer is: "The people come and go and draw from the well. If one gets down almost to the water and the rope does not go all the way, or the jug breaks, it brings misfortune."

This is the responsibility. Accordingly, it is entirely up to the individual to decide how much of nature's unlimited energies he is able and willing to appropriate. I mean to say that here the will is primary, because anyone can do what he wants to do; of course, not in the sense of finishing tonight what he wants to complete tonight. But whatever an individual wants to do from within the depth of his soul, this he will fashion. By this I mean that our whole life, experi-

enced today as event, is the result of previous acts of
the will. To be sure, the product does not always coincide with the intended result. Indeed, the results of
many of our wishes differ from their intended consequences. But the end results always from developments that occurred in accordance with fixed laws.
We all have the rope that reaches the depth of life.
We all have the jug with which to draw water. This is
how we are constituted as a body-soul unit, and as
such we are a part of nature and have contact with nature. Our contact is with the matter and forces of
outward existence, as well as with life's fullness of the
soul. Therefore, it is important to come and go and to
draw. Therefore, it is important to repeat the creative
act anew each time. The creative act that penetrates
and fashions inanimate matter produces tensions and
results in works and forms. We call it diligence; the
characteristic of every genius. For it is not greater talent that distinguishes the man of genius. Many of our
greatest geniuses were outstanding neither for their
talent nor for their effortless activity. Mere talent
without diligence must sooner or later become trite.
The characteristic of the man of genius is that he acts
in accordance with his being.

Therefore, we must attend to the two aspects concerned with how to draw on the energies of life at our
disposal. It is important to see to it that the rope does
not stop short of the water, without actually reaching
it. And it is also important that the jug does not break,
even though it is used time and again to draw from
the well. This is the secret. For should the jug break,
the saying will have been correct. And this we do not
want.

Exactly what is meant that the rope must reach the
water? Ultimate life forces are universal and free,

available to all men. The greater and more important a life force, the more universally accessible it is. Embellishments and adornments of life, treasures and conveniences, available or unavailable, these are costly and only for a minority. Things least necessary are most expensive. But the daily bread that we need to remain alive is cheap. Water is still more vital than bread, and is even cheaper. Air, however, without which we cannot live even a minute, has no price; all men can have it whenever they want. Air is available to everyone. And should bad air ever suffocate a man, it will not be because there is no available air, but because he cannot, or does not want to, reach a place where air is accessible to all. To a still greater degree this is true of life. Air is matter. There may come a time when we are in a place with bad air, or no air at all, which we are unable to leave. But life penetrates everywhere; there is no place without life. Remembering this force, life comes. Thus a human being is one with life, has life and is effective in life whenever he wants.

At this point we must clearly differentiate between the life of the soul and the life of the spirit. Material life is tied to material conditions. Material conditions are finite and limited. We cannot have them the moment we want them. But spiritual life, and this is essential—spiritual values that are significant of life— these no one can take from us. An army can be deprived of its general, but even the most insignificant person cannot be deprived of his will. Fire and water and other things can or cannot be obtained. Such things may even be dangerous. But life "humanness," wherein lies the value of man, is always present. The moment I want "humanness," life at its highest, it is here. An individual who appropriates "humanness" has life; essential, valuable, spiritual life. And such life is obtainable.

Therefore, it is, of course, important to work. Even though life is present everywhere, it is always and only accessible, as it were, when experienced as transparent. We must have things through which life can glimmer, although this precisely allows people to mistake superficial things for ultimate values of life. These superficialities are, however, only crystallized life, and crystallized life is life in the process of withering away. Solidified and having become torpid, such life cannot endure. If crystallized life satisfies us—this means if we are content with any type of social structure, with petrified customs or habits—our rope does not reach the bottom. Not everyone can fetch his own water. There are people for whom it must be done. They live by and are sustained by customs. This is good and proper. They belong to the multitude and we must not condemn them. There are, however, others who are destined to give life; they, so to speak, draw from the well. To such people we should belong. Therefore, our responsibility is that the rope reaches the bottom. We must be thorough and absolutely truthful. We must penetrate that which is apparently only so and be satisfied with nothing less— may it loom ever so large—than with the actual source of life.

This is hard and sorrowful work. If customs and habits were to satisfy us, life would be easy. We would do as others do, and what happens to others, happens to us also. We have no problems, nor do we have the hurt of isolation. But if we are driven by unquenchable thirst to draw at the spring, nothing else will suffice and we have to pay the price. Everything in this world has its price, including drawing life at the spring. The price is suffering; suffering that necessarily guards the gate there, where an individual reaches the titanic decision to break through beyond what all think and do, and to face eternity.

In addition to thoroughness, practicing perseverance is also important, for the jug must not break. Now we experience mysteries, revelations, and, to be sure, many frightful things. Life is not as simple as people think it is. In the well are dangerous animals. For is not water at once the image of danger? Only the person who perseveres in danger continues neither hastily nor fearfully to penetrate until he has passed the threshold's guardian; only that person who faces hardships does not break the jug. And therefore, only that person can raise life into daylight.

For such a person the well is his character's sphere of activity. Life thus obtained immediately from ultimate depths is not only his, but can be transferred to others. Those who drew once from the spring of life are people who received the call. They do not draw life for themselves. They do not seek to keep it in their jug and drink from it alone. Were this so life would become stale. Here is a law that differs from the law of matter. The law of matter is: the more I collect and the more I store up, the more I have. But the law of life is: the more I distribute, the more I disseminate, and the more I contribute, the richer I am. Therefore, it is important that those who once had contact with life become in turn the source to which others might come and go to satisfy their life requirements.

The first line of the hexagram moves, admonishing gravely: "One does not drink the mud of the well. No animals come to an old well." Of what use is a well with mud instead of water? It is not a well. There are people who once drilled wells, and were in touch with life. But then they devised systems, and the systems became muddier and ever more tedious, and the muddier the system the prouder they were. They wrote volume upon volume, and finally the system became a support by means of which they groped their way through life. Suddenly they find that no animals come and the water is not tasty. To go beyond one's own system, to surpass oneself and become renewed; to seek life at its source and not collect it in an old cistern, this precisely means not to become mud that is useless for restoring living beings.

Our task, therefore, is not to permit the effort to vex us. No matter how often we are disappointed, we must try to start again. Then this divine thirsting, this divine yearning for the springs of life will remain alive. And such yearning can never be disappointed, because its goal is not to find any one thing. Its direction is tension, and as tension it signifies energy. Life neither can nor should satisfy. Always in motion, always striving forward, reaching out for the new: then even hardship, even misfortune, become a source of strength. Hardships are deadening only when they are immobile. However great a burden, if it moves it is a source of strength. However great a suffering, it is a moment of advance as a result of which there is progress. The person whom God intends to be great and whom he entrusts with a mission is first thoroughly tormented. God opposes him and obstructs his plans. God tires out his body and persecutes him with sickness and with pain. And because of this a man's spirit becomes pliable and his nerves strong. Such a man is able to approach life wherever he meets it.

The hexagram Ching, the Well, ☵☴, becomes

Hsü, Waiting, ☰☰, when the lowest line changes.
What are the benefits of having decided in difficult
times to perceive and grasp life at its source? The answer is: Waiting. Waiting is also composed of the trigram water above, but below there is Heaven. Wood,
which penetrates, is now closed below, thus changing
into the Firm, the Creative. Waiting means integration into the context of nature. We must not expect
that the coming year will only bring blossoms and
roses. Quite likely we should anticipate having to wait.
Clouds are gathering in Heaven; we cannot make
rain fall, we simply have to wait for it. Eventually it
will rain, and this is precisely the characteristic of
waiting and patience. We know it will rain. We know
we will reach our goal, no matter what the danger;
our inner strength is equal to overcome it. This is
Waiting. "If you are sincere, you have light and success. Perseverance brings good fortune. It furthers
one to cross the great water."

The inner light indicated by the hexagram makes
the strength creative that has been drawn from the
well of life. But now there is danger, and we must
compose ourselves; we must not run blindly into
danger, but hold back, even as a noble steed is restrained from leaping. Perhaps this position should
be assumed in the coming year. At first we should re-
strain ourselves and realize that we cannot advance as
we would like.

We must learn to wait with strength. Most people,
while waiting, become either bored or melancholy.
Neither is patience. Nothing is more revolting than a
form of Christian patience, which is really no more
than resentment. The individual has resigned himself
to accomplish nothing, and seemingly submits. Such
submission, however, indicates that one meets every-

thing critically and spitefully, and burdens all motion as if with lead. But leaden, burdensome patience is not waiting. Waiting is tension. Waiting is certainty, not only a possibility. That which we expect will certainly materialize, it will absolutely and certainly come about; we know it as internal necessity. Waiting is not externally conditioned, because all real value is unconditional. And, being unconditional, we have strength to wait, which helps to be truly patient in various situations.

The individual lines of the hexagram show the many ways of anticipating danger. One person remains in the distance. He waits on the meadow and holds to the old ways; danger is still far away. Another waits on the sand by the river; there is some gossip, and the shadows of danger appear in advance. The third waits in mud which, to be sure, is an unfavorable situation. It is uncomfortable and hastens the enemy's arrival. The fourth waits already in danger, that is, in blood. The text states: "Get out of the pit." The fifth waits at meat and drink: "Perseverance brings good fortune." The sixth waits in apparent destruction: "One falls into the pit. Three uninvited guests arrive. Honor them, and in the end there will be good fortune."

We would be led too far afield, were we to describe all the situations in detail. At the same time, we should divest ourselves of illusions about the difficulties ahead. Therefore, we ought to preserve an inner gaiety. The superior man waits at meat and drink, he waits until it rains, for rain it must. Indeed, this we want: to preserve inner joy, unconquerable in sorrow, need, or disappointment. Such joy is not based on shallow optimism, and is independent of hormonal conditions that may lead to playfulness: this joy comes from within. And, therefore, it may very well be related to battles of the soul as well as to dire and difficult distress. In fact, at the time of greatest distress, in times of isolation, when one no longer knows how to move, then joy sets in, this "nevertheless" that is invincible.

SHAPING

The situation begins with the hexagram Hsiao Ch'u, The Taming Power of the Small. This hexagram is composed of the Creative, Ch'ien, ☰ , within or below, the image of Heaven; and wind, ☴, the image of the Gentle, of the organically shaping, passing over it. The function of wind is to tame creative forces, to accumulate these and to make them visible. It is exceedingly difficult to understand this relationship of forces, because the power used here is not expressed with might, but it is the softest, gentlest, force imaginable. Wind is the least visible of all temporal phenomena, and this invisible wind is now needed to concentrate that which strives upward, the strongest of all phenomena. Hence the name "The Taming Power of the Small." For Sun, the Gentle, is the oldest daughter and is small; Ch'ien, the Strong, is the father and is great.

The judgment reads: "The Taming Power of the Small has success. Dense clouds, no rain from our western region." And the image is described as: "The wind driven across heaven: the image of The Taming Power of the Small. Thus the superior man refines the outward aspect of his nature."

Further analysis of this situation reveals an element that corresponds to our present time. Today we confront tasks that tax the limit of our strength. We must tame the great by means of something small; concentrate it, shape it, and make it visible. To be sure, in varying perspectives this is a problem in every environment. But, in beginning with the greatest, a turning point is reached in the history of mankind where new creative forces are stirring and strive upward to the surface. What will become of them; how are they to be shaped? We are the ones whose task it is to concentrate and to shape these forces. This is the task of the generation at the turning point. However, while this generation confronts gravest responsibility, it lacks the superhuman energy required for the task. For is it not a characteristic mark of our time that there is a lack of heroes, of great men, whose excellence is such that they create new cultures out of nothing? Mankind today is average. We all feel responsibility, all of us are aware of the task, but no matter how great our longing, the leader we long for does not appear. It may be that the essential aspect of our time is—and perhaps this is the task—that something new and creative can no longer be built around the personality of an exceptional leader. Such a person might carry within himself again too much of the human element, be too human. Instead of shaping and crystallizing the infinite, he would produce only something of finite value. The present generation then confronts an extremely difficult task in this situation. What is to be? How is anything new—as it emerges from confused and chaotic grounds—how is it to be merged with existing phenomena?

On the one hand, this process has the obstacle of every formative process that is related to the difficulty of matter generally. No one finds it easy to master matter with spirit, for matter is eternally heavy and spirit is eternally powerless. But the process also has obstacles of a wholly different nature. We cannot give shape to anything yet; the time for definitive creativity has not come. Chaos has still not ceased. Therefore, we must calmly and sincerely admit that it is wrong to work at shaping something definitively before a maturing point is reached.

If, for example, we look to China, in this connection, we ask with anxious concern: what will be? What is the shape of things to come? Where is the point, the goal, that will coincide with reality? We search. In China, too, people search. First one man emerges, and then another. Every so often a great, strong, movement arises, firing the hearts and hopes of people, that something will be formed; but soon everything collapses again, and new shapes emerge from the chaos.

Does this mean that there is no possibility? That nothing can be accomplished? No. It merely means that the turning point has not yet been reached. Our bows must be stretched further, and more substances and more forces must be absorbed. What we have to build is a broad, large form, in which everything will find a place. Work of this kind cannot be prematurely concluded because the forces denied active opportunity would explode the structure. Only after the maximum point of expansion is reached in a form so great that all surging chaos finds its place therein, only from within such depths can shape be given.

Although this obviously applies to China, it is also applicable to all mankind. Movements cross hither and thither; Asia is awakening, the nations seethe in Africa, and white mankind suddenly is sucked into a process of dissolution. The Westerners' special position, which they sought to maintain for centuries to come, suddenly disintegrates. What will be? Where is this great form, an all-encompassing form in which everything has a place? Confronted by this, the spiritual energy of patience alone, as we have seen, prevents despair; time and again inner certainty that something will be, gives us courage and hope. With this in mind, we will be able to assume the proper position regarding these problems.

These problems do not demand forcing the issue. That which is not yet ripe internally must not be forcefully concluded. We must learn to wait. But waiting is not inactivity. In waiting we need not remain idle. We must realize that this is not a time for concluding, nor is it a time for perfecting. Ours is a preparatory time. Realizing this, we must work at that which must be worked at. This is the work of details. It never reaches greatness. Therefore, the text: "Thus the superior man refines the outward aspect of his nature." Minute work is precisely necessary in times of waiting.

Nevertheless, it somehow sounds strange that we are to refine to the utmost the powers within us. The meaning is that giving shape to the chaos within us is work confined necessarily to the individual. Refining the outward aspect of being prepares the ground for the new becoming, for all chaos must be refined before it can be given shape. The task of refining must begin with the external aspect of our being—for there is the point from which the world can be moved. Indeed, the world cannot be moved from the center of the soul, from the seat of the unconscious. The unconscious acts and creates as it must, and we should submit to the surgings of its waves. Only in the peripheral region, in the small free zone of consciousness, can work be taken up each day, and whatever needs refining can be refined. This is not superfluous work. Although this small zone of consciousness and freedom is only a thin rind, its contact with the forces of the unconscious is vigorous. We may think of it as similar to the brain, which is covered with a thin, gray layer. In this thin gray layer of conscious reflection is the point where progress takes place. From there, the borderline is pushed ever further into unknown lands as we anew appropriate the world. Hence, that which is seemingly small and insignificant is, after all, the power that succeeds in taming chaos by means of steady work and perseverance, even if nothing is given shape. Working in small matters on ourselves, we must also radiate strength to the outside. This is not the time to form associations or schools to cultivate the new secretively and in isolation. Rather, in radiating the inner light we should join those with whom there can be mutual understanding. Such alliances must leave open a door so that the force of our nature can be made known to the fullest extent. Let there be no more esoteric doctrines, closed to exoteric teachings, but let us keep the borders flexible. That which is inside must constantly overflow to the outside, in this way alone will the new be prepared; new paths will appear, enabling us to practice spirituality. And eventually we will reach the proper time when sorrow will be terminated with lightning speed, and creation will be completed. All creation is sudden, as if from Heaven, and not a gradual collecting. Creation is qualitative, appearing completed one day. However, we must not assume that we merely need wait for the sudden event. Instead, our task is to prepare the atmosphere, to satiate it with possibilities so that the spark can penetrate. It is always so at first; the atmosphere must be charged in preparation for the creative spark. And this slow preparatory work is The Taming Power of the Small.

A great and difficult task awaits us. No sphere of activity is too small. Each sphere—alloted by fate and matured with us, which we did not choose arbitrarily—each such sphere, regardless of its label, is the place of work where the Taming Power of the Small concentrates the Creative.

An additional aspect is presented: "Dense clouds, no rain from our western region." This image refers to the era of King Wen, the founder of the Chou dynasty. He lived around 1100 B.C., when the Chou dynasty, in the west of China, still suffered from the oppression of the last tyrant of the Yin dynasty, Chou Hsin.[5] This tyrant's control was oppressive. Although King Wen had within him the potentiality for creating order, he did not succeed in externalizing this potentiality. In the western region, the Chou family seat, clouds rose to Heaven, rain was imminent, but did not fall. We should realize the tragedy of King Wen's position. He saw what must happen, but he also saw himself stopped by circumstances. King Wen knew that he must live and die without accomplishing a thing. One man comprehended the depth of this tragedy, and that was Goethe. It is indeed striking that his small diary notation, "O Ouen Ouang" (Oh King Wen), occurs at Goethe's most difficult time in Weimar. He obviously had read about King Wen's situation in Jesuit translations of the period. From these he understood that here was a man who knew what ought to happen, but who was persistently stopped and oppressed by conditions that he could neither remedy nor overcome with the obviously necessary actions. This small notation is the poem "Ilmenau," compressed, as it were, into a sigh.[6]

The result is clearly understandable. Here, too, it is the small, impotent, and spiritual that must succeed against strength and unspirituality. It can always and only tame and limit, and is incapable of overthrowing the great and powerful. It can only prevent the worst; tame and limit to the extent that at least a future becomes possible.

Such work is thankless. For how to work always apparently unsuccessfully, how only to tame? To answer, this work is the basis of success. Precisely because of the superhuman patience of the Chou dynasty's founder, the dynasty rose like a bright sun on the horizon; Chou culture became the greatest China had ever seen, and the effects of this culture were felt for millennia hence. China became China because of the heritage of those formative eight hundred years, when the Chou dynasty occupied the throne. And although King Wen's superhuman patience accomplished nothing visible at first, it nevertheless tamed and limited. External detailed work and refinement created the basis on which later great creation became possible. Such men as King Wen are the vanguard fighters in mankind's divine struggle. They never see the harvest, they may glance only from afar into the promised land. Indeed, most often others gather the fruit. But such fruit as may be harvested is sown by the vanguard. The harvest's success is prepared at the height of renunciation, at the time of small battles of resignation and limitation.

Fortunately, there is still another aspect, one that transcends that which is conditioned by time, and is related to that which is essentially human. Let us look at the hexagram more closely. Below is the Strong, Creative, which is not always gentle and mild. Creative forces overflow, are transforming—the Creative is also revolutionary. The trigram Ch'ien is in the northwest of Heaven, and the text states: Heaven battles the beings in the sign of Ch'ien. Ch'ien is a battling trigram; it is judgment, as well as the autumnal winds that rush through decaying branches, flinging to the ground everything unable to live. This is creativity, creating through destruction, in continuous crisis so that something new can originate. These coarse and demonic aspects must be transformed and must become visibly apparent in the phenomenal world. These are coarse, wild, confused, and invisible powers that are perceived in creativity, in chaos. But what is it that will give these powers shape? It is gentleness and impotence, seemingly unable to imbue with form.

In the *Book of Changes* two hexagrams deal with this problem. One hexagram is Lü, Treading; with Tui, the Joyous, following the strong and Creative. This however, is not an attempt to give form, but is proper conduct in joyous submission to omnipotence. In our case the task is larger. In addition to joining in joyousness, the issue is to make visible strong and dangerous aspects. And here is a wonderful image of wind blowing over Heaven. In spite of being invisible, formative forces continually rise to Heaven, into the atmosphere. But now the wind, cool and moderating, blows over Heaven. The vapors having risen upward in the heat, reappear as cloud, as fluid image, and not as inflexible wall. However, what commands the step from invisibility, from the unconscious, to visibility? It is precisely the cooperation between the Gentle, penetrating, and the Strong, moving. Here, then, is the ultimate operation of light and dark forces, masculine and feminine, or whatever other name we want to give to this cosmic polarity. One pole has the powers and surges forward, the other causes them to appear in seemingly gentle adaptation. But the effect of this gentle adaptation is indeed mighty, for it exposes the forces so that clouds appear in Heaven.

And the effects of the Gentle upon the Creative? This question touches upon a complexity indicated, for example, in "Faust" by the image of the mothers. With the mothers is nature, the eternally feminine. From within it emerge the images of everything. The Creative, "the greatest of masters," who helps the weaving maiden, is the first to assume a dim shape in these images.[7] The idea is the point where spirit and reality commence to touch one another. The idea is as yet not a graspable reality. But it differs from a purely spiritual, intellectual concept. And being no mere fantasy, the idea may be considered as the creative energy in the process of forming. Hence, the point where we experience this event, the image in the process of forming—the incomprehensible, ungraspable image suspended in nothingness—the point of timelessness, of greatest loneliness, which forms the center of the world, this is the point where we experience that event which is designated as the Taming Power of the Small. Still, even here is a way that leads to all situations. For when we see cosmic powers take effect, we recognize them to be the same as those manifested everywhere where something is formed and becomes reality. Everywhere one pole presses forward and the other endows it with image and form, for activity to take place. Our soul works in this way, and this is how all parts of our soul act together. One supplies energy, the other form.

But here, too, is a peculiar relationship. The image Sun, wind, the Gentle is diametrically opposed to the Creative according to the order of the diagram of the

Later Heaven, or the world of appearances. Ch'ien stands in the northwest, where life struggles with death and it acts in this struggle as the Creative. Sun, on the other hand, stands in the southeast, where beings enter form (are brought to completion) once the Arousing has started its motion. The godhead makes beings enter their forms in the sign of Sun. And entering into form is precisely the power that tames the Creative and leads it to appear. Perhaps this is a magic, magic in its highest and ultimate meaning; the forces of the world are always interdependent, and by acting together produce something new and essential. All work originates in this way, real work and not mechanical output. For this is the path of all becoming: it grows and contains life within.

But even this is difficult. Even this necessitates incredible self-effacement. Self-denial is exactly at the point of transition where form and content combine into shape, and when form must disavow itself. Form that does not cling, that does not give itself up, and does not die, cannot fulfill itself. Only when transcendental form relinquishes itself, can ideas descend and the word become flesh.

An interesting aspect of this hexagram is that the line which gives the border point and must be considered with special care is six in the fourth place. It is the only yin line in the entire hexagram, and as such it should control and tame the remaining five, strong lines. The entire coherence and responsibility rests on this one, weak line. It has no power; power is attributed to strong lines. But precisely, therefore, it must know how to subdue force with gentleness. And how will it happen? "If you are sincere, blood vanishes and fear gives way. No blame."

Even here is something similar to tragedy; the

struggle of a new Becoming is not simple. The new always takes shape in blood and fear. It takes shape by passing through the point of indifference we usually call death. On one plane something has to die, so that on another something can take its place. Therefore, utmost sincerity causes blood and fear to vanish. One line in the entire hexagram is different; it subdues the Creative and finds itself sacrificed. It must relinquish itself, and be at the disposal of others. When a person reaches a certain stage of development that is most difficult, he rebels when it is demanded that he renounce himself. He does not want to relinquish in renunciation precisely that which he feels as his very own, even if it is to be passed on, even if its purpose is to form something new. We do not wish to be deprived of our best forms. But the new cannot be given shape in any other way. One planet must be shattered for a new world to arise. A person must die so that he can become himself; he must relinquish and renounce himself, in order to rediscover himself in infinity. In life's process it is essential not to stop here. Most people go as far as this point only. But when the limit and its ultimate loneliness is reached, and when one, as it were, confronts infinity, there to affirm and relinquish oneself, that is a gain; but a gain won in bitter combat.

Let us once more return from these human, metaphysical, contemplations to historical perspectives. For therein lies the task of this generation. Our generation, in whom the past still lives, must be ready to sacrifice itself. We should not try to safeguard the most precious possessions of the past as they exist now; we must not conservatively protect from destruction the beauty we have come to love. Beauty thus preserved would only stagnate and petrify. No matter how painful, we must prepare to move forward into the new time, together with old remnants that tradition has given us—unsentimentally, bravely, and hopefully. Once this decision is reached, then the new time will take shape. New times must remain in contact with old times. Humanity must not experience a break. Otherwise history would be meaningless. Future means continuity of the present, possibly an intensifying, but continuity nevertheless. The abyss between past and present is closed by the generation that represents the past; that knows the old treasures and yet is prepared to sacrifice these and to cross over into the new world.

At first, this new world is not beautiful. There never was a new world that was beautiful. When the Christian Middle Ages separated from the world of antiquity, how many irreplaceable goods were lost then; how much beauty disappeared underground, together with Greek art; and how poor and unpleasing were the new goods, how proletarian and ugly! But they were new, and only because people carried over the old treasures, adding these to the hot molten mass, only therefore did new innovation grow beautiful again. And so it is also in China. How infinitely beautiful is the Chinese past! Is there indeed, anything greater, or more pleasing than Chinese wisdom of life? We must, however, not stop with such happiness. This is the past; instead of seeking it in otherworldly contemplations, we should prepare to take the hand of the new and leave behind the old. Our duty is always to plant loyally the field of time, planting it with the experiences of holiness and greatness. And what is to become of it? This is left up to the field.

And something will become of it! Because when

man has relinquished himself, he rediscovers himself in infinity. Therefore, The Taming Power of the Small, which, as such, represents hardship and a superhuman task, is also the turning point: blood and fear vanish, the New is here, the Creative. When the fourth line, only a turning point before, now changes from a weak line into a strong one, the entire hexagram becomes uniformly strong, and we have the hexagram that marks the beginning of the *Book of Changes*: the new concept, Ch'ien, Heaven, the Creative, ☰.

This development is deeply meaningful. And looking back, we now understand that there is no other way when eras change. There is no other way than bravely passing through death and sacrifice to prepare the new Becoming: the outgrowth of the two poles of the past.

The Creative confronts us: "The Creative works sublime success, furthering through perseverance. The movement of heaven is full of power. Thus the superior man makes himself strong and untiring." This is the promised land into which we may take a look. Yes, indeed, it is the new era. The new era should be creative, not a time of ruin, neither a vacant echo of a dead culture, but an era that will transcend the old culture. Two characteristics are associated with the Creative; one is primary, or sublime success. The Chinese character for the sublime is the head. But the character does not only signify the head; it is also the most vital, the deepest aspect permeated by complete sincerity and genuineness, the cause of itself—success that comes from within. This acts creatively. The other aspect, concealed in success, is perseverance and the grace of beauty, which is joy. To understand the Creative in this connection, we are

shown again the central meaning of the transition
point, though it must be remembered that we are not
speaking of the Creative as such, but of the shaping of
the Creative as a result of the situation. The point of
transition contains the complete fullness of that which
is eternally feminine. According to the *Book of
Changes*, the eternally feminine unfolds as three
categories, called daughters, within the world of appearance. The oldest daughter is Sun, the Gentle,
Penetrating, the Wind, the Organic. The second
daughter is Li, Flame, Clarity, Brilliance. And the
third daughter is Tui, the Lake, Gladness, the Joyous.
These three forms of the phenomenal world: first the
penetrating, then the clearly luminous, then the joyous resting within itself, are three grades of development, inherent in the power indicated by the fourth
line. The great success of the Creative in this difficult
and responsible position is aided by these three.

The hexagram conceals within it several trigrams:

To begin with, there is the lower trigram, Ch'ien,
Heaven, and the upper trigram, Sun, the Gentle,
Penetrating. If, however, the uppermost line is discarded, a new trigram is formed. We have now one
strong, one weak, and again a strong line. This trigram is Li, phenomenon, Clarity. One line lower we
have one weak and two strong lines. This is Tui, the
Joyous, the Sea. Thus the hexagram conceals the
entire succession of the yin principle, as partial or as
nuclear trigrams. The creative process occurs in this
order. By gently penetrating, by the idea assuming

image, light and clarity emerge, and the goal is seen. The goal is seen as it were in Heaven as the sun, and in such sunshine neither murky twilight nor dark mysticism exists, but in their place is clear and conscious action. This also is characteristic of our time: after we have crossed over and perceived the idea, we must be entirely conscious. We must be conscious because our era, the anticipated new era, will not take the form of earlier cultures, when unconscious elements pressed from below instinctively and animalistically. Humankind has reached the point where, by taking the future in its own hands, it must recognize clearly what to do next. Thus we will find the way to that which is divine within us. This is the second step.

The third step is beauty: Joyousness. Joyousness, so to speak, exists where the way is seen. Then everything is easy, all difficulties are overcome, joyousness sheds its radiance, and here is the place of art. Even as a woman's task is to beautify life, even as she was at all times considered the priestess of beauty, so also here is a task, hers for all time. The effects of this principle are always different. Art must create, must become active, but in beauty. This is perhaps the only point that always differentiates feminine and masculine work.

We are not talking about woman as only an empirical phenomenon, as part of humanity, but rather of the eternally feminine, which is a part of all of us. The effects of this eternally feminine aspect are precisely such that by attracting us, we are led into depth and led out into clarity. Perfect beauty, then, is that which transfigures everything that the power of the Creative made appear in the phenomenal world.

New power originates thus. Everything that has entered the phenomenal world in this way has power.

To be sure, spirit is more impotent than anything else in the world; spirit carries no weight and has, therefore, no material power. But it is also true that spirit is more powerful than anything else on earth when creatively concentrated, and when the tension-producing goal is such that it produces an attraction. The thrust of the goal is then not external, but illuminated; all beings come to it. And the result is as the commentary to the Creative predicts: the Creative causes all beings to enter their forms; it causes the rain to fall and the shapes to emerge; it causes the saint to appear and all men flock to him. This is the result of the struggle, and the era for which we are responsible. Such prospects prove the struggle worthwhile, and we need not despair. And even though we see the hardships before us, we may also hope for eventual success.

DEPERSONALIZATION[8]

We saw that constancy in change is actually an aspect of life as such. Life does not rest, and it is not rigid, but like a fountain eternally rises and eternally falls. In its rising and falling lies its constancy. We saw that constancy in change also has its origin in the Taming Power of the Small—in the idea, the Creative becomes visible. That the Creative visibly appears occurs in accordance with constant laws. Nonetheless, constancy in this case necessitates eventual sacrifice. That which can cause the Creative to become manifest must vanish again, as if melted down into the creative process. Its last effectiveness is only a stimulating energy, active in the New, which is to be. It may be thought of as the bridge that is built in this way from the past to the future. However, these reflections would not be complete if we were not to consider a third aspect of constancy in change, an aspect that brings us very close to reality. The Taming Power of the Great,☰☰, is a hexagram that seemingly differs little from the Taming Power of the Small. The Taming Power of the Small had the Creative, Ch'ien, Heaven within; and Sun, the Gentle, Penetrating, the Wind, without. One weak line sought to tame and hold together the entire hexagram, even as wind tries to induce the precipitation of rain clouds by blowing over the heavens. In this hexagram, however, there is one more yielding line; two yielding lines, one in the fourth place and one in the fifth place. One firm line above, then the two yielding lines, and below again three firm lines; the Creative, Heaven below, and above, this time, the Mountain. Hence, there is a vast difference between the two hexagrams. This difference is not only indicated by the presence of two yielding lines instead of one, which might indicate an increase and therefore an easier wielding of power. No, within the form itself lies the essential difference. Above is the Mountain, the Keeping Still, hence something very real: Heaven within the Mountain.

Among old legends of many peoples we find time and again the idea of a Heaven within a mountain. Time and again we find the thought of something massive, strong, and high that contains a cave, and within the cave Heaven. Heaven as different from the world of the day, and yet as a world filled with creative power. This world is endowed with the capability of giving shape, and sooner or later it enters the created world to usher in the Golden Age. The notion of a cave-heaven occurs not only in our German legends; we find it also in far away Asia.

All such legends are frequently, or almost always, a

metaphor for something that takes place within a human being. This is also the case in this hexagram. Heaven stands for human creative powers. These creative powers are here tamed, held together by the strength of Keeping Still. The creative powers that are surging outward in time are restrained by a very strong inhibition; and by being restrained in this way they are forced to form, not only to become idea, but to continue forming until they enter reality.

The text to this hexagram is: "The Taming Power of the Great. Perseverance furthers. Not eating at home brings good fortune. It furthers one to cross the great water." And the image: "Heaven within the mountain: the image of the Taming Power of the Great. Thus the superior man acquaints himself with the many sayings of antiquity and many deeds of the past, in order to strengthen his character thereby."

Everything depends on surmounting subjectivity. The creative power within us is to be given shape when used in such a way as to make it objectively fruitful. The following is probably indicated by the image: the lower of the two yielding lines has its origin in the negative pole, and signifies the emotional powers that can stimulate, as the wind that blows over heaven. They are, however, very mobile, they come and go and, therefore, do not lend shape to anything. As stimulation they merely rage like a storm; then they disappear and everything remains as of old. Therefore, the emotional element alone, the vegetative aspect of feeling, is never capable of creating anything enduring. It stimulates, begins, but cannot complete.

The upper middle line is the subject. It is in the place of the sovereign, on the border of consciousness in the human being, and its consciousness is in the form of the I. But the I as such is also not powerful. It is like the beam of a flashlight, illuminating the process of emotional movement, and focusing it sharply in the light. Caught by the beam of light, things seem to transform and change, whereas the beam alone appears to endure. But it, too, cannot endure. Because the scene that it illuminates is also always different. Moving in front of us is a ceaseless stream without end and without beginning; new waters forever appear in the light, emerge in a burst of radiance, and then disappear. Such is the I that appears so secure—endowed, as it were, with wisdom's conclusive finality—and yet is so transitory. In fact, we even feel how this I changes in the course of the day. Only the circumstance that we can imagine a continuity ascribes something enduring to the I. In reality, though, not even this relationship is found within time. There are always longer or shorter moments in life when consciousness is suspended, when we sleep, dream, or are unconscious. At such times life goes its way, fusty and untouched by the beam of light. We wake up once more, and something retained by memory allows us to resume where we left off. Thus we join the new into the old, and, accustomed to overlook the gaps, an ideal picture of the I, enduring through changes of time, is constructed.

The Buddha recognized this deception perhaps more clearly than anyone else. He recognized that this is the point where all suffering begins. Here, then, is the eternal contradiction. Because the I is entirely incorporeal, it owes its beginning solely to combining with something else. A schism is necessarily connected with the I, because the I falls on something, without a light of its own, and makes it transparent. What is it that we designate as our I? Is it the body, which will undergo complete transformation within only a few years? Is it the processes of the soul, which have no more permanency than the bodily processes? Is it love, is it hate? Greed? Abhorrence? Such feelings come and go; joy and pain forever replace one another. A tendency appears to be present, however; everyone wants happiness and everyone seeks to escape misfortune. But even this tendency seems to exist only toward the end of binding the human being so much more to transitoriness. Wanting happiness and shunning unhappiness, fear and hope, are feelings that embitter life most. They rob us even of the one moment, when one's I has at least reality. They rob us of the moment of the present, and, instead, throw us back onto the past with its ghosts or its magic images, while withdrawing them at the same time as the paradise lost. Or they drive us forward, toward a future devoid of attributes and obscure, which hurries forward out of the darkness and gains momentum at the very moment when meeting the I with its light. There we rush ahead with our thoughts, and we fear and hope. And because of this, the last point, the point where it is possible at least to enjoy the second, also disappears.

Therefore, the Buddha conceived the idea of the illusion of all life. But not illusion without substance, rather illusion whose major characteristic is suffering. The I does not exist, it is merely composed of complexes of the soul's states which, when they become transparent and equipped with a distinctive mark, consider themselves as existent. And while the I is as nonexistent as ever, it is nevertheless now imprisoned in transitoriness. In itself, transitoriness is not suffering. Each moment is separate, and be the moment ever so horrid, a second later it has passed. Each moment exists, neither as suffering nor as joy. Nonetheless, the wheel of suffering is kept in motion because of the craving and greed of the I. The I is willing to accept the nourishment of transitoriness, that is, to nourish itself from illusions. To be nourished by illusion is to resort to nonnourishment and, therefore, craving is created anew each time.

The Buddha thus reached a daring conclusion. With psychological sagacity and unconcerned thought, with an energy unknown to us Europeans, he analyzed this entire I-complex. His reflections led the Buddha to create for himself an instrument so sharp and so cutting that nothing of any extension could resist. Salvation comes to the Buddha because this nothingness acquires the power to dissolve everything that exists. The very moment when the I is dismembered, we know that it is not I that is dismembered. It is a sort of feeling that comes and goes; a process of life that belongs to the beginning of craving and nourishing, and is the cause of new craving. We recognize it as unreasonable, clinging, flowing endlessly from the depth of the waters. By creating this thought process, and with the incisiveness by which the Buddha dissolves all existence and all life, the I ceases to be. Without the I, material existence may still continue for a while, as perhaps a potter's wheel turns for a time after utensils are no longer made on it. But the circular course has ended. Salvation has come.

The concept of life expressed here is very severe. It is not a concept we can dismiss in two words. It is an abyss into which we must look bravely for once, in order to discuss these things altogether. Unless a person is prepared to follow the Buddha's thought, to toil and to descend all the way, he will be unable to

replace the Buddha's concept with another, because
the Buddha's concept is the most radical and the most
ultimate.

Still, in the *Book of Changes*, there is another concept. This is not, to be sure, the notion that something
spatial or temporal endures in change. That change is
without beginning, is endlessly, infinitely reproductive, is as clear to the *Book of Changes* as it was to the
Buddha. Moreover, that things come and go, and are
not real, but momentary embodiments of something
else, is obvious as well. The *Book of Changes* also acknowledges, as does Chinese wisdom of life generally,
that when a person permits things to make of him a
thing, he will suffer. Then he is pulled into the
schism, because a person is not a thing but a subject,
and now he suffers as an object suffers because he has
identified himself with the object. Such is the source
of suffering. Nevertheless, there exists a point at
which the Buddha's teaching can be overcome. Actually, this should be expressed more cautiously, for
the Buddha's teaching cannot be overcome. We can
only confront it with another teaching, as justifiable as
the Buddha's, and which, in turn, cannot be overcome either. There are two possibilities, and I hardly
believe there is a third. The two ways are ultimate al-
ternatives of existence, and the individual must
choose the road that fate and character dictate.

Let us look closer at the hexagram we are dealing
with.

We discussed the lower, fourth line, and described it
as the weak line of vegetative life, of emotions and

feelings. We also discussed the fifth line as another essentially weak line of subjective experience. The line still remaining to be discussed is the uppermost strong line. This line is Heaven, the Creative, Law. The vegetative life of perception and feeling, and the subjective oscillation between fear and hope and whatever flows from this are subordinated to a master. The master, however, is now no longer subjective, but the objective; Heaven, the Creative, or however we may want to call this force. By forming this kind of organization, Tao (or whatever its name) becomes master over the human and temporal element in the human being, and there emerges the shape of a trinity, solidified within itself: the Mountain, Keeping Still! Nothing that is transitory can endure. But that which is objective—humanity ruled by Heaven— possible in all of us, this can endure. As an organism that neither power nor time can dismember, it is an enduring movement coined in form, and not rigid. And in spite of being impressed with form, it flows with life.[9]

This is the secret. And this is the power symbolized by the mountain, which grasps and gives shape to the Creative. The Chinese consider the mountain a cosmic phenomenon; not merely an accumulation of earth and stones, but a center—we might say a center of magnetic and electric forces. Something happens on and around a mountain. Life congregates, vapors rising from earth condense there; from the hood of fog that covers the mountain rains dash down to earth to make earth fruitful. Plants and trees grow there. Birds come to the trees; field animals live there. A living organism covers the mountain like a thin green skin. We must always sense these meanings when speaking of the Chinese concept of the mountain. These are ideas of strong solidity, Keeping Still, which endure for a long time, much longer than the life gathered about it, and providing, therefore, the opportunity for shelter and security. The delicately flowing stream of life is given stability by the mountain. Keeping Still contains three ideas. First is the idea of solidity and security offered by the mountain. Second is the idea of gathering, which arises because of this solidity. A mountain standing in the atmosphere collects and gathers about it the forces of life. The third idea is one of nourishment and benefit. Life settles in and about the mountain, and the process of life continues. All life rejoices in the mountain's solidity, and the great power of the mountain nourishes all life.

This most obvious of all mysteries, the mysterious manifestation of the mountain, is an ultimate expression of the hexagram. Mysteriously and yet obviously, the mountain nourishes, gathers, and strengthens life. Life in turn is represented by the image of Heaven resting within the mountain, and as shaped by the mountain in the valleys around it.

With this image in mind, we can now deal with the problem mentioned earlier: is there constancy in change? Is there something that can save us from despair? Is there something that can lead us to agree with life if we do not wish to take this irrevocable step of renunciation the Buddha has taken, and do not want dissolution into nonbeing? Here is a point, which links the Far East with the West, and which we can accept, namely, the acknowledgment of life and the rejection of asceticism as a negation of life. Moreover, we can agree with that which within us accepts life, provided we shape it with an instrument that will cause it to become eternal and enduring in change. We must adapt to objectivity. But not capriciously, not with our ego, the small ego, formed in day-to-day needs. Nor is such adapting the reflection of something that our body manifests as reflex in our nerves and brain. By objectivity is meant that which is neither here nor there, and yet is here and there; the human being who is not "I" and who is not "you," and yet is within me and within you. It is the human being who is neither today nor tomorrow, and yet exists both today and tomorrow; the human being who was here from the beginning and who will be here until eternity. It is this great Being, in which we do not participate—indeed, such an expression is entirely wrong—but which we are, because humankind is I and I am humankind. Nevertheless, the stipulated condition is at once something more than any one human being, any one time, or any one place in mankind's great relationship. This is the Lord, Spirit, which all religions have sensed, and have toiled and struggled to express. They may call it the Lord in Heaven, and with this project Him above the clouds, because He is higher than anything else below. But precisely, therefore, He is removed from the world and adored from afar, He is condemned to nonexistence. He becomes the image of man projected into the emptiness of universal space, an image to which we seek to give life with the sap and energy of our own lives. Or He may be called the Messiah, Christ, who walked among us as the representative of mankind. These are images that we experience when we experience the human being within us. Yet man is not a sum, he is not a multitude of individuals, he is not a majority. Instead—and this is the mystery—man is manifold as well as uniform, expanding in time and space as many single individuals. And when we live to leave this isolation, searching to find its basis; when we return from the rays of the great sun mirrored in the fragments of the mirror to the source of the rays, we find Tao. But not the Tao of Heaven nor the Tao of Earth, but the Tao of man. There we find objective law, which is constancy in change.

Constancy in change supplies our psychic structure with the energy for taming the naturally creative aspect within us; to shape it, to take it under our care, and to nourish it with that which is necessary for life. Collecting and concentrating—thus our nature becomes rich, strong, and shining, nourished and supported. As a result, the entelechy of the individual can reflect eternity within, and each individual life, inseparable from eternity, acquires shape and meaning within eternity. Goethe said once: "We are not immortal to the same degree." Each person is immortal, Goethe felt, as far as he succeeds in giving eternal meaning to his life, and becoming transparent for the eternal man whose overwhelming greatness reaches the greatest distances, and is at the same time so small that it may be found even in the smallest place.

Hence, The Taming Power of the Great is indeed contained in this hexagram. It is a rich, an important, a great and beautiful thing, because it is good. No need to choose in a petty way; we can stretch our bow as far as we can, until it reaches Heaven itself. We can now encompass everything within us. Perhaps one of the greatest of Confucius' ideas was precisely this teaching of The Taming Power of the Great, which is capable of taming the entire human being. Neither the amputation of limbs, nor the removal of anything within us is necessary; instead we can accept ourselves as we are. We can accept the Heavenly primary aspect with which we have arrived in this world. We can accept and love our virtues, and we can enjoy them as well; and we may also love the animal within us, if such a daring word is permitted. The law must be so great as to shape everything. Because, indeed, what is the animal in us? What is this that we designate as bad, as urge, as sensuality, this pejorative that we term "sin?" What are all these? They are obstacles in our nature, that do not fit into the harmony. However, there are two ways of approach. Either we are too weak and cannot be the master in our own house; then the animals must be thrown out and we must go into the desert, withdraw from our environment, as did St. Anthony, only to have the animals return more frequently in our dreams. I cannot believe that a man ever really succeeded in separating himself from his animals. Indeed, psychoanalysis performs its most important function when it uncovers the zoo within us, and when it simply leads us into this society and says: now, behave yourself and get along with this animal world. They are also you; if you want to kill them, you will kill with each one a part of yourself. I say: Confucius' greatness is that he tames without killing. He does not prescribe anemia by means of asceticism. To be sure, even the most bloodthirsty lion can be tamed for a time by depriving him of food, but taming by starvation is not real taming, because as soon as the lion is free he will devour even more. Therefore, the other approach is perhaps deeper: to take oneself as one is, to be gentle with oneself, even with these wild animals, greeting them and recognizing them as part of oneself. But the next task is to let the animals know that they are not the master. Confucius' strength lies in that he tames; the beast is not freed, but is held in check. Success consists in creating order; by ordering high and low, important and unimportant within one's own person. Everything, the least significant as well as the least pretentious; the lowest as well as the most common have their rightful place. Somewhere each thing has its spot. Our sins also have their places when they are subdued. Sins have value, for they are sources of strength; they must pull the wagon in the direction designated by the wise leader. Therefore the problem is to so harmonize the energies within us that the great can become great, and the small can become small. Never must the small be in the master's place, and the great languish unredeemed below. But everything must have its place for Heaven to be enclosed by this strong Mountain.

Through this comes redemption. Sins are converted into powers. And the human being ceases to be a sinful creature, for he is enabled to attain a place, beyond sin, where Tao prevails. Confucius' approach in the *Book of Changes* is to point out the method that will lead to this end. Mencius said once: "Every man has great sides and small sides. The great man identifies himself with his great sides, and the small man identifies himself with his small sides."[10] This is all there is to it. If we identify ourselves with our best powers and begin from this point to shape and to tame, then there is progress.

And here is another secret: the taming cannot occur by means of wild force. Again we deal with something delicate, the two lines—the fourth line as minister corresponds to the world of sensations, and the fifth line as master corresponds to the personal world. Both, although weak—for what are purposes and emotions—now wax powerful, because they are fitted within law, and because they voluntarily help to make law effective. Thus law is enveloped by beauty. Neither a gloomy "ought" nor a harsh "must," law now leads to pleasure; because attractively equipped, we are prepared to obey it freely. Such is the secret of proper conduct.[11] It would lead too far afield to amplify in this place. I only want to point out that proper conduct, voluntarily complied with, is both the law of beauty that attracts others, and is the power that tames the Heavenly as well as nature in us.

From this arises possibility. According to the text, "Perseverance furthers. Not eating at home brings good fortune. It furthers one to cross the great water." Not eating at home means not to adhere to the I. Out, where people live; do not remain within the petty I, revolving in its small orbit; but go outside, into the ferment of life, into the raging battle of life, where potentialities are found and shapes are formed; there to be nourished, but not by bread and water, or meat and vegetables alone. We want to be nourished by spiritual movements, from the Creative, that demands forming. From this to draw nourishment, the power to collect and to gather, to grasp what moves and to give shape to chaos. This is the task expressed in these words. Therefore, it furthers to cross the great water; therefore, it furthers to undertake the ablutions, this holy bath of purification, so utterly necessary if the soul is to enter the divine grove of Heaven. Indeed, there are rich possibilities in this hexagram. We see man outgrow his little I, we see him grow into the world where he acquires constancy in change.

The image points to just this: "Heaven within the mountain: the image of The Taming Power of the Great. Thus the superior man acquaints himself with many sayings of antiquity and many deeds of the past," because in these, too, the human being is found. This is neither traditionalism nor false conservatism, but is objectifying the law that always was and always is, the law that determines existence, in order to make his character firm. When the two lower lines of the hexagram, The Taming Power of the Great, ☰☰, change, we have Ken, Keeping Still, the Mountain, ☶☶.

The configuration of The Taming Power of the Great undergoes a basic change because the first two lines of the hexagram move. The text of the first line is as follows: Nine at the beginning: "Danger is at hand. It furthers one to desist." And the second line: Nine in the second place: "The axletrees are taken from the wagon."

If that which we have learned so far were not clearly realized, these two sentences would be very discouraging. The two sentences indicate that our present as well as future circumstances are not conditions of great, free, and unobstructed activity. According to the first sentence, danger is at hand; better desist. Mankind has times of day and times of night. During the day it is important to act, because when night comes no one can act. This is a truth that is not pathetic. Night, when no one can act, is not eternal, it is neither hell nor death. Rather, night is a time when life, as it were, flows subterraneously, when it withdraws from conscious influence, when obstructions are signals to keep still. The body similarly has signals, expressed as pain. These direct attention to wherever an illness is, and lead to the awareness to keep still, allowing the healing forces of nature, time and rest, to take over. In life, likewise, signals appear, warning us that danger is at hand. We must acquiesce; not only because it is written in the *Book of Changes*, but reality itself, the time toward which we are moving, is one of danger. Astrology also designates it as such, and reasonable and sober examination of the circumstances confronting us show danger signals arising everywhere. Hence wisdom dictates that we not attempt their denial. To be sure, nothing is more comforting or more pleasant than to ignore danger and attempt to break through. But this is possible only if the danger is merely transitory. There are men whose inner elan suffices to take to the trench, provided the trench is narrow enough, and to make possible that which seems impossible. May the person prosper who has not killed the inner flexibility that allows him to deny danger, in order to overcome it. Such a person has a valuable and divine gift that he must treasure. For only he is young who maintains this treasure. Others, however, ought to be prudent and understand the signals. Especially if the danger is not merely momentary, surmountable with one's own energy, but is, as it were, an objective world configuration. Then our strength must not be wasted, we must be thrifty. Danger in an objective situation cannot be overcome. This is nighttime. And anyone who is then unnecessarily active, as if it were day, cannot be effective; he will injure himself and others. Hence the second line: the image of the wagon. The wagon wants to move forward. The wagon, the wheel of the wagon, is the symbol of Heaven below. Heaven, the circular, wheel-like, which rolls and is self-moving, is the tendency to move ahead, because the Creative, concentrated within it, urges forward. But now the wagon's axletree must be removed. This is not joy, this is renunciation. We must have great self-control to acknowledge that here is a time of waiting, a time when the axletree is to be removed from the wagon. It is a voluntary action. Another sign says: the wheels fall from the wagon.[12] But we fortunately do not have to face this danger, we are given an opportunity to adjust to the new situation. Still, the situation is grave, because the movement ceases. The Creative below turns into Keeping Still: Keeping Still above and Keeping Still below; mountains standing close together. That which the mountains mysteriously know is now present in concentrated form. And, therefore, the text to hexagram Ken reads: "Keeping his back still so that he no longer feels his body. He goes into his courtyard and does not see his people. No blame." And the image: "Mountains standing close together: the image of Keeping Still. Thus the superior man does not permit his thoughts to go beyond his situation."

This is productive Keeping Still. For the mountain in China is considered a place of death, but also as the place of newly originating life. In our hexagram the northeast is represented as the place where life and death, day and night, touch one another. Still, how is it possible to hold fast to constancy in change in such difficult times?

Above the entrance of the Maulbronn Monastery are two interesting markings in the form of two peculiar rosettes. Sculpted into the stone above the double

gate, they are akin in type, and yet are entirely different. One rosette represents a tendril, and in its execution the movement is seen as constant rotation; the
rosette next to it has blossomed into a rose of the
cross, a blossom in which the divine line of the cosmic
cross is shown. The cross still contains its powers, but
they have come to rest; resting in viewing, resting in
tension. I do not know whether the monks at Maulbronn considered the issue in this light when they put
up these curious rosettes over the gate. Had they
perhaps wanted to indicate a return from the chaos of
life to the quietude of the monastery, as the higher
sphere of meditation? Whatever the reason, the
thought expressed here is profoundly meaningful. It
represents two possibilities. Represented here is bustling life that can come to rest, a rest signifying a concentration of energies. This is an outline of viewing,
final internal viewing, when the human being is no
longer aware of his back, when he comes from meditation exercises. The I has, as it were, disappeared,
and the person begins to view the deeper layers of his
personality, and in such internal experiencing he
reaches unconscious levels. Moreover, he also "goes
into his courtyard and does not see his people." This
is a vision that gives shape to that which is objective. It
is a vision such as Orestes had, when he suddenly
looked up in a moment of madness and saw the terrible fighters peacefully before him. In this vision he
saw all of the figures that had injured and killed one
another walk peacefully together, and in his sorrow
he saw, as if in a flash, the mighty and eternally calm
Immobility.

Therefore, the task is indeed significant. We must
close the gates for the internal vision to occur, and in
Keeping Still, raise up the mountain within us. And

although we rest a moment, it is neither death nor cessation, but a transition from old to new. Whether the new year brings hardships and battles, whether it brings dangers, or urges us sometimes to remove the wagon's axletree, we must not become despondent and discouraged. Instead, we want to keep free of the unrest that such dangers might produce. In fact, we should confront the divine moments of the inner vision time and again, because they bring rest, which is life-producing and result in concentrating tension.

Thus we cross over from the old to the new. The sun's solstice may give us new energies for whatever is in store. We hope to find the energy to shape it actively and vitally, according to the laws that assure constancy in change.

Death and Renewal

According to the Chinese concept of the world, all phenomenal existence is conditioned by two polar contrasts, the contrasts of light and dark, the positive and negative, or yang and yin. In the metaphysical realm, the contrast appears as life and death. It is not mere chance that one of the oldest Chinese documents tells that the happiness promised to man is finding a death that will crown life—*his* death. And the greatest unhappiness that threatens man is a premature death; a death that tears life, instead of completing it. It is obvious, therefore, that precisely this dark aspect that accompanies the light is not only something negative and opposed to life, but its very presence and its shape determines at once the light aspect of life. It was not just through caution or superstition that the ancient sages did not praise a person as happy before his death. For it is a plain fact that the meaning of life is derived to a degree from what is outside life—this dark something that we go to meet.

However, in order to focus on this, we need a certain amount of courage, and no one who still fears death has a right to speak of death. We must become accustomed to cultivate fearlessness; a fearlessness that prepares us to face everything we encounter, and to come to terms with whatever the future might bring.

The question now is, what can China tell us about this problem of death? To begin with, the problem is differently presented. Previously, in Europe, life and death were regarded as two antithetical sections of time of unequal duration. Life was rather short. It could last seventy, eighty, or even one hundred years. Life began in time, and notwithstanding its shortness, was essentially meaningful. On life depended whether a person would spend all eternity—eternity conceived as ceaseless time—in heaven or in hell. This concept was probably derived from Persian beliefs, and was accepted by Christianity together with certain Platonic influences. Generally today this concept is felt to be unsatisfactory, although we do not seem to have a more satisfactory concept with which to replace it. We affirm as real one half, that is, the brief life here on earth; but the half that follows we regard with doubt. In the East, however, the concept of reality is somewhat differently distributed between the two halves. Life, the half that appears so important to us, is, as it were, divested of its glaring sunlight. Life is not as real as we take it to be. For reality in the East means, in the final analysis, only appearance, that is, reality merely within the polar duality mentioned above. And if, on the one hand, life is not seen as solid, the shadowy world of death, on the other hand, is also not seen as purely negative. The time of night is included within the great context of life and death. This is taken so far that life and death belong in equal measure to the world of appearances, while existence lies beyond both.

It is generally assumed in the East that whatever has a beginning must also have an end. Life, which begins in time, must end again in time. Similarly, whatever ends must also begin anew. Life, having ended in time, will be resumed in time. Expressed here is the idea of circular change, which includes day and night in equal measure and, therefore, contains also life as well as death. This circular change is familiar to us in nature. When we see the leaves fall in autumn and the vital saps withdraw from the tips of the branches, we know for certain that this end will be followed by a new beginning. Sun and spring will return, the sap will rise in the branches, and new leaves will sprout in place of the old fallen ones.

This general view of life and death prevalent in the Far East leads to various explanations intended to give meaning to human life. Let us take first the Confucian concept. Although Confucius most certainly contemplated these matters, he expressed his views guardedly. When questioned by his disciples about death, he said: "While you do not know life, how can you know about death."[1] Another time, when a disciple asked whether or not the dead were conscious, he said: "Were I to say that the dead have consciousness one might fear that filial sons and obedient grandchildren would neglect their live relatives in order to bury the dead. Were I to say that the dead have no consciousness one might fear that undutiful sons would leave their parents unburied. Wait until you are dead, then you will experience it."[2] Therefore, Confucius' standpoint is to have the common people remain in doubt and tension in such matters. Neither dogma nor creeds of faith, but personal dignity should determine their behavior. The inner imperative will lead the people to act properly. Thus we see that Confucius generally rejected such questions. He refused to construct a dogma, but wanted to encourage a free shaping of moral behavior independent of mankind's two greatest enemies, fear and hope.

Nevertheless, it should not be assumed that views on death are entirely absent in Confucianism. To the contrary, we find some very clear conceptions. Through sheer ignorance we have come to regard Confucius as a rationalist, who, by means of a solid, bourgeois, and somewhat homely morality, has led millions of Chinese through the centuries. Time and again this image of Confucius reappears and, indeed, it seems almost indestructible. Possibly this is so because a misunderstood Confucius was imported to Europe at the time of the Enlightenment, and it was this image of Confucius that was very highly esteemed. As times changed, this picture of Confucius has long been respected.

What, then, are the views of Confucianism on death? They are found in the so-called "wings" of the *Book of Changes*, attributed to Confucius and his school. These wings present the concept of a phenomenal world of polarity that may be designated as Heaven and Earth, or light and dark. These two principles are described as "Looking upward, we contemplate with its help the signs in the heavens; looking down, we examine the lines of the earth. Thus we come to know the circumstances of the dark and the light. Going back to the beginnings of things and pursuing them to the end, we come to know the lessons of birth and death. The union of seed and power produces all [living] things; the escape of the animus [and the sinking down of the anima] brings about the decay of life. Through this we come to know the conditions of outgoing and returning spirits."[3] The union of seed (seed as the image-like, idea-like) and power (the substance-like, shape-imbuing) produces the beginning of living matter. On the other hand, we have also something else. This is arising consciousness (animus, *hun*), which contains as if formed in advance the primal image of the human being. The union of preformed consciousness, or the spiritual, with nature (power) produces the life of the soul. This union, however, is not a mixing, but a formation of polar tension that causes, in turn, a type of rotation. Hence, the life of the soul moves continually about these two poles—the pole of power and the pole of consciousness. The rotating movement attracts the elements, shaping them into forms that correspond to its nature. The characteristic of all life is this basic duality. It is said that when the child utters the first cry, the two principles, which were once united in the mother's womb, separate, and for the rest of the person's life they will never find each other again. From now on consciousness is the viewer and the knower. Deeper down it is the experiencer, and in the deepest depth it is that which feels. And from there it reaches into the lowest regions, the realm of power—the organic. But consciousness has only indirect access to this organic realm, which is by no means a compliant tool. The organic realm is a tool with which spirit—higher though less powerful—must struggle. From this we can understand clearly that consciousness and power separate again. "The animus escapes, and the anima sinks into the depth." This is death. At the very moment of death both principles assume different aspects. During life, they lead a deceptive unity in the body, for the person (persona, actually the mask) is, to the Chinese, the body. The body is the unifying bond of the various powers of the soul that are active in the human being. But within this unifying bond they always act as variegated powers. And only the sage succeeds in creating harmony by taking his standpoint in the center of the movement. The body disintegrates in death, and simultaneously the deception of unity ceases. The *Book of Documents*[4] describes a ruler's death at one point as "Ascent and Descent." The two principles are so constituted that one, the soul of the body, the anima (*p'o*), descends; and the other, animus (*hun*) or more spiritual, ascends.[5] As the elements separate, whatever descends is subject to dissolution. Together with the body, the anima also disintegrates. Disintegration, however, is not simply destruction. While in the process of decay, the bodily components are thought to be subject to reorganization. They do not disappear. They may, in fact, enter into different organic combinations that are later absorbed by other organic substances, prior to complete exhaustion. The assumption is that the bodily soul consists of unities of a different kind, which are not subject to complete exhaustion, and even though they sink down together with the substances they once governed—thus naturally ceasing to constitute a personality—they still somehow can be regarded as tendencies or powers. Together with the dispersion of material elements, there occurs also the dispersion of psychic elements that once more prepare to reconstitute themselves. The process of reconstitution is not difficult to understand. The broken-down remnants of death nourish the succession of life, and in this way organic components transfer to new life. This results in the widespread Chinese concept that it is the soul of the land that permeates man. The components of life entering and leaving the earth are powers that also influence the development of the human being. It is as if there were a reservoir of life, imbuing the whole with a distinct and clearly defined atmosphere. The idea that the dead who are not entirely broken down organically have the power to give shape is so strong that it even surpasses the notion of race as thought of by Europeans. To be sure, the

Chinese also take the parental heritage into consideration. But this inheritance is always connected with the great continuance of the primeval ancestors who now rest in paternal soil. Hence the belief that a Chinese ought to be buried in his native land. Where he hails from—not only as material body, but also as psychic construction—to that place he wants to return. And therefore, even those Chinese who have divested themselves of their Chinese heritage and who serve in foreign countries may save their last penny so that their remains can be returned to the native land. For this reason, too, Chinese are subject to frequent and morbid homesickness when far from their native land and when separated from the mother ground. Hence also the ecstatic joy when a Chinese comes back to China. I once saw the poet Hsü Chih-mo[6] as he returned from a year's absence in Europe. I will never forget his exclamation: "Here this earth, here these rivers, here these trees; this is my flesh and blood, from this I came, from this I live, and now I am home again!" One realizes here that life, decay, and death form a successive cycle that is not theoretically taught, but immediately experienced.

In addition to this vegetative soul, the corporeally alive, there is still another soul, which I designate as the animus. I do not want to say it is a higher soul, for this would be a qualitative evaluation. Rather, it is the intellectual, spiritual; or still more clearly, that which is spiritually receptive. Spirit as such is not something that the human being can produce from within himself; it is something that is acquired in the course of life. And perhaps life exists precisely in order to be imbued with spirituality. According to the Confucian point of view, this spiritual soul contains after death some sort of consciousness. The onset of death is not total annihilation. Just as the body does not decompose at once, but retains its form for a time, so does the psyche. The two elements separate; one remains with the body and the other separates from it. However, somehow a relationship with the body is retained, so that a certain degree of perception remains. Thus, for example, the deceased hears what is said in his presence. It is, therefore, customary in China not to speak ill words in a deathchamber. Everything should be said as if the deceased were present, so that, without being disturbed, the separation from the body can be concluded.

Generally, dynamic conceptualizations are prevalent in China. The Chinese do not emphasize "substance" as mass; "substance" in China is rather conceived as a state of energy.

Although spirit, therefore, does not exist as substance, we must not regard it as nonexistent. It is, as it were, a tendency of consciousness. To be sure, as such it leads a somewhat precarious existence—unless, of course, it was so concentrated in the course of life as to permit the building of a subtle body about it. A body of thoughts and works, a spiritually constituted body, to provide a support when the dissociation from matter—the helpmate, now prevented from offering further shelter—takes place. This psychic body is at first very delicate, and only the greatest of sages find in it a support beyond death.

For ordinary people the survivors must furnish this support. This is the significance of ancestor worship. The sacrifice to ancestors means precisely that pious remembrance permits the psychic element to dwell as if in living substance. Each good thought sent on to the departed gives him strength and prevents his being scattered into nothingness.[f] As a rule, it is not assumed that this life—even though it does not end with death—is eternal life. Rather, it is visualized as a gradual disappearance into twilight, a second death. Because descendants remember their ancestors only as long as the ancestors' living tradition is present among them, more genteel families sacrifice to more generations than do the common people, who seldom remember more than four or five generations. Here still another idea may be involved, namely that the ancestors return to this world after they have lived for a while in the other world. Already in remote antiquity a succession of generations appears to have been assumed, where one generation skips the next, and is embodied in the following generation. The grandfather, for example, appears in the grandson. This, however, must not be understood as a mechanical process. For the grandson is not the actual person of the grandfather. Instead, the idea must be conceived as taking place in a series; something of the grandfather's generation, something of his manner, lives in the grandson. But not merely as accidental resemblance; rather, part of the grandfather's vitality actually appears again in the grandson. Therefore, it is believed that the ancestors return after a lapse of time as if to a general and spiritual reservoir from which they will sooner or later unite once more with human bodies and human souls as their stimuli and impulses to life.

[f] This idea is very similar to the one advocated by [Gustav Theodor] Fechner. The basis of his idea of immortality is as follows: after the primary body has decayed, the body of immortality is formed in the thoughts of other men. It is formed by their remembrance of the deceased. Hence, it is as if a body of a higher grade develops, in which the deceased can continue to live.

Such is more or less the idea of Confucianism. And the only exception is that all human beings are not viewed as equally immortal. Whoever has harmonized his nature and caused his existence to be so effective as to emanate powers—we may call them magical powers—because they transform and act creatively, such a person will not return after death. He will not be *kuei*, but a *shen*. *Shen* means someone divinely effective—man as hero, who is connected with the entire cultural complex. The duration of the culture is also his duration, because his life endures in the pantheon of this culture. To this very day Confucius is thought of as being present. And not only Confucius, but other great men, such as, for example, Yüeh Fei,[7] the loyal knight without fear and blemish. These are only the greatest of men. They succeeded in putting their given entelechy into constant rotation by being securely and creatively anchored within the cultural complex.[g]

We advance a step further when we realize how Taoism deals with this problem. Taoism considers the human being as not essentially different from all other life. A person is merely a special species of life; indeed, a somewhat bothersome species, because a person is endowed with the dubious gift of consciousness, and, therefore, is capable of follies, whereas all other creatures live and die naturally and on their own. For Taoism, the problem is something else. The rhythm of life is simply entrance and exit. Entrance is birth, exit is death. And because the rhythm of entering and leaving takes place continually, Lao Tzu says:[8]

[g] Goethe also expressed this idea. He declared once that he was convinced we are not all immortal in the same way.

> See, all things however they flourish
> Return to the root from which they grew.

This root, which is at once the germinating seed, is eternity, is life. We read further:

> The Valley Spirit never dies.
> It is named the Mysterious Female.
> And the Doorway of the Mysterious Female
> Is the base from which Heaven and Earth sprang.
> It is there within us all the while;
> Draw upon it as you will, it never runs dry.

Lao Tzu here refers to the waterfall of life; a waterfall of showers spraying in the sun. The waterfall is composed of always new drops, and yet its form is constant. Not because the drops are constant, but because the conditions that guide the drops in their course remain constant. Thus the soul of man is like water; water that comes from Heaven and rises to Heaven, and is formed by Tao. This is the destiny of man.

From this point of view, the immoderate importance ascribed to life and death appears in fact like a misunderstanding. Hence we find that Chuang Tzu[9] faces death with unencumbered heart,[h] and most other Taoists regard death as easy farewell. Even though consciousness disappears in death, consciousness to them is not of primary importance. On the contrary, it is a festering wound causing one to suffer throughout one's life. Finally, when in death consciousness ceases, it is as if the ropes of someone suspended by his feet had been loosened. But for this to happen, the concept of the ego has to be transferred.

[h] Compare *Chuang Tzu*, Book xxvii, 20 [in the Richard Wilhelm translation. In the Chinese original the reference is to the last section of book xxxii].

For as long as I identify myself with this transitory body, I will suffer with whatever is transitory in the body. For then I erroneously suppose that I disappear in death, whereas only the components surrounding me separate again. Therefore, the problem to Lao Tzu and to Taoism generally is to expand the I (ego) from transitoriness to ever wider spheres—to the family, the nation, mankind, and the world. And finally, whosoever can walk together with sun and moon has an existence that will endure as long as sun and moon endure; and whosoever has reached the state beyond becoming lives eternally.

Although the concept is the same as in Confucianism, in Taoism it is separated from human circumstances and is transferred to the entire life of nature.

Buddhism goes still a step further by identifying life with suffering. Our intention here is not to present the views of Southern Buddhism, for Southern Buddhism has long been known in Europe, but it may be well to show the rhythm of events as expressed in Northern Chinese Buddhism. A person at birth is not a substance, but a fusion of states of mobile matter. It is something like a whirlwind that whirls up dust. The whirlwind of dust appears to exist in space, but in reality it is no more than a state of atmospheric pressure that causes ever new whirls. As new winds enter the whirl, new dust particles rise into the air, and so the whirlwind of dust assumes the appearance of enduring existence. This is the human being as long as he lives. He is a whirling movement due to a variety of material and psychic causes. And without being an actual substance, the movement endures, because necessarily one state follows another. Birth is followed by development; man takes nourishment, grows, and matures; then comes love, sickness, old age, and death. But the course does not stop here. For as long as the causes are not exhausted, and once the cycle is visible, the succession is repeated over and over. Just as whirlwinds may become invisible in dustless places, new dust is whirled up as soon as they enter dusty regions. We call it the transmigration of souls, or the succession of births, although neither of these expressions is entirely correct. According to the Tibetan concept, the soul moves through three successive states after death. Therefore, death masks are always strangely transfigured, at least those that represent peaceful dying and not death in horror and shock. Death spreads peace over the human face when, for the moment, the world of appearance disappears. Nothingness, which nonetheless is beyond Something and Nothing, appears momentarily. If the deceased succeeds in remaining with this instant he has reached Nirvana. But only few are capable of this. Most persons sink one step lower, where images of consciousness come to them like dreams. At first come good images, the divinities. These divinities, as it is explained very clearly, do not exist within themselves, they are only emanations of one's one heart seen now as if existing externally. It is very interesting to observe the psychic breakdown, for after the good divinities come the terrifying ones. But these terrifying divinities are not to be feared. They are the same powers as the good divinities, only now viewed from a different aspect. Good divinities are emanations of the heart, evil ones are products of the brain. Both are produced from within the person and should be neither loved nor feared. Actually, they are only temptations that approach in order to lure the human being again into the phenomenal world. Then comes the second step, as the breakdown continues. The person turns away from the past. Now the results of life's deeds take their effect; at first only in the psychic realm. These are the hells and heavens as intermediary steps. Indeed, only Christianity knows eternal punishment in hell, thus most cruelly betraying its founder. But even these psychic results of our deeds gradually break down. The soul sinks farther and farther into twilight, and consciousness is increasingly lost. The whirl remains, at first, intact, only it is as if without nourishment. It is an airwhirl without dust, and therefore the soul begins to feel wretched. He who has not found the entry to salvation now hungers and thirsts for existence. Although he feels the state of dissolution, where everything corporeal has decayed and one layer after the other has fallen off, his thirst for life has not ceased. As he strives toward renewed existence, man again approaches the real world. Wishful images appear.

And wherever on earth a child is conceived, hungry souls crowd closer and through the mother's body seek entrance to new birth. To be sure, birth necessitates the union of the masculine and feminine poles in matter. But this alone does not produce a new human being. At the moment of union one of these existence-thirsty souls must be there, ready, as ever, to thrust its way into life. For this very reason there are so many unwanted children. Children do not come according to the parents' wish; they come according to the wishes of these unhappy souls. In wild delusion souls force their way in, intent on new existence; for it is delusion that drives them on.

Europeans frequently consider the doctrine of reincarnation as exceedingly reassuring, because it imparts the conviction that one may return again to the world. But this is not the Oriental view. Transmigration is the great burden under which Orientals suffer. Neither life itself nor happiness of life is the focal point, but death. The moment one enters into life, one must face death at its end. Hence, one is born to ever-new deaths; one is always born to face the monstrous and dreadful end. And one must endure it over and over, until one is released. Here the concept of karma enters the picture, which is that these souls select suitable future bodies in correspondence to their nature. A reincarnated person, therefore, is not simply a repetition of the past, since corporeality now consists of altogether different elements and forms, and only previous impulses are still present. Rather, a reincarnated person will have selected suitable physical abilities in order to materialize best his central tendencies. Thus it may happen that a man who was a jewel thief in a past life might be a jeweller in the next, or someone who was cruel may become a lion. It should not be supposed, as we are accustomed to think, that these are matters of punishments. Karma, in the final analysis, is not an ethical doctrine, but it rather means that every tendency seeks lawful intensification. This intensifying endures even beyond individual existence; it endures to the point where the great return ensues. This point is the release when delusion ceases. And where delusion ends, there is Nirvana, there is the great peace. Nirvana, in this sense, is not a purely negative concept; Nirvana is a higher state than the state within polar tension. It is a condition of oneness, and those who exist within polar opposites can understand it only with great difficulty, or not at all.

II

The concept of life as a movement, time and again interrupted by death, is decidedly a problem of scientific interest. However, this problem has still another aspect due to the special fact that we are not dealing here with a process observable in plants and animals, a process that takes place in the external world, or in psychological experiencing. Rather, unique psychic connotations accompany life and the concept of death, for it is I who lives, and it is I who conceives of the death of my life. Hence precisely this consciousness of myself endows this problem with singular tension. Clearly life, like any other creative power, is so constituted that it does not contain within itself sufficient reason for cessation. Therefore, all living creatures have by nature the love of life. The power that causes the cessation of life is opposed to life. Obvious, then, is also life's instinctive fear and fright, as long as it is life, when faced with its cessation. In addition, a person is so constituted that consciousness is not only related to this circumference of psychic phenomena, called life. Consciousness means a mirroring of what takes place in the brain's complex, and perhaps also in other areas of the body, on an incorporeal plane. Hence, connected with the circumference of psychic phenomena is the fact that this consciousness is precisely *my* consciousness, that we are conscious of ourselves.

And what is the I? This is the greatest riddle. We may compare it with a light point moving forward in time without expansion in time. What it is, we cannot explain, we can only experience. We all know what differentiates the experience of the I from all other experiences. And this I is now tied to a complex of life events and identifies itself with these events. I am my body, I am the sum or harmony—whatever else I want to label it—of events that enter my consciousness as my body's life events. Hence, love of life is not an anonymous power, but it is my love of my life, giving the problem an entirely new aspect, because it is my fear and reluctance to have life cease that demands solution.

In dealing with this problem, we must be calm and strict. The issue is not that we think great thoughts and feel strong emotions when confronting death. Experience has shown that these help very little. Indeed, the strongly articulated feeling does not necessarily coincide with reality. We frequently have strong feelings that have no relationship whatsoever to reality. There may be people who have died most beautiful deaths—soaring as if on wings of exaltation from consciousness into unconsciousness—but who were far from gaining victory. The question is simply, what about life and what about death? Is it possible to overcome death? And if we are able to overcome death, what are the ways that will actually lead to it?

In answering this question we realize at once: the modern attitude to physical life must be completely sanctioned. The medieval attitude, which regarded earth as a vale of tears, and which advocated escape from life, was a type of self-deception. It could be maintained only when coupled with fanciful fantasies of future heavens, where one hoped to soar from this vale of tears. Today, however, we realize that the asset we have is none other than our physical life. We do not have at our disposal a second or another life. We also know that to all true religions the life in the body, the soul-body unit, is of great importance. This is not only a modern, materialistic idea since even original

Christianity also emphasized bodily life with regard to man's fate after death. And although the goal of Buddhism is to release the person from everything called life because all life is torment, Buddhism, too, accepts physical life as its only weapon in the struggle. The conclusion—and this conclusion is always drawn in the East—is to value, to respect, and to care for the life of the body. The senseless absurdity of dying, which has no basis in life, may very well have led in antiquity—and perhaps not only in antiquity, but always—to attempts at abolishing death; to attempts at prolonging life infinitely. Although such attempts cannot be refuted logically, they do not interest us particularly here, because until now—in ancient as well as in modern times—all committed the mistake of the "absurdity of dying," of experiencing death on their own bodies. However, there is something to these attempts that may not make them entirely meaningless. True, we may not be sufficiently advanced to boast justifiably about consciousness when facing death. We have not yet learned to die; we have not yet reached the point where we would, so to speak, not die sloppily, but die as it befits to die. For this reason I say: without having reached this point, we must secure as much time as is needed to reach this stage in our life cycle. Because should we die prematurely, and should the death, therefore, not be a proper one, then whatever comes after, also cannot be proper.

Attempts to prolong human life were carried out in the various philosophical schools, such as Buddhism, Taoism, and even Confucianism of the Sung dynasty. They were not only designed to prolong a person's life to perhaps seventy or eighty years, but for much longer spans. The starting point of such efforts was

the initiation of accurate observations through intro-
spection about the processes of life, and the factors
that either further or inhibit life. Accordingly, life
blood, or life in the blood, is assigned a significant
role. Time and again it is stated that water is important to the soul, and that the fire of the spirit must
penetrate this water in order to prolong life. "Water
and fire do not combat one another" is an old magical
saying from the *Book of Changes*, which contains the
secret of life. This, in the final analysis, is simply the
idea of baptism; the baptism by water, and baptism
with the Holy Ghost and with fire. Hence secret religions in the Orient advocate a method aimed at prolonging life by making the blood healthy. Blood is to
be freed of its sediments and its congestions. All
obstructions are to be overcome so that the blood's
circulation can be constant and unimpeded, and by
flowing continuously never fall behind the times. According to this concept, blood is not merely a mixture
of chemical substances, but it contains the soul elements: "Blood is a very special fluid." If blood is dissi-
pated externally, the soul may be scattered and life
consumed. Meant here is not only the external loss of
blood; internal dissipation of life matter, too, can
cause this. This same blood, on the other hand, this
very special fluid, if allowed to take its internal course
unobstructed, is exactly power acting on power. For
the human being, blood is the substratum of the soul,
the substratum of life in the body.

What, then, were the methods for prolonging life
through cleansing, consecration, and renewal of
blood? There are in China certain meditation exercises that are very interesting when regarded in the
light of recent researches. The external form of their
directives calls frequently to mind alchemical pre-

scriptions. Means are listed for melting the pearl of life, the gold pearl, the stone of wisdom, or whatever else the elixir may be called. Although Chinese alchemists occasionally prepared medicinal substances, which were by no means rejected as long as they were effective, we must not think of Chinese alchemy as a science of chemistry. Chinese alchemy is a psychic technique. The point is to activate certain psychic centers, at rest in ordinary life. Because they cause the cessation of life by not functioning, these psychic centers are to be activated by concentrating attention on them. But what does it mean, "concentration of attention?"

The answer leads to a secret of the entire practice. We know that attention is subordinate to our will. This means that it is up to us to direct our attention to the point to which we want it directed. But we are also aware that such an act of the will uses up an infinite amount of strength, so that more than a mere directing is barely possible. Hence, the power to fix attention does not come easily to our will. To be sure, we might force the fixing of attention, but such results as might accrue would be unproductive and would amount to nothing. Rather, the fixing of attention must be guided independently of intention. Undirected attention is not power. Only a directed, as if concentrated, attention signifies in psychic life something really creative, power. And such attention must be directed to the life centers, toward this system of activities that keeps the blood in motion so that the centers awake, begin to move, and thereby cause the renewed beginning of life.

At this very point the magic power of the image is put into practice. For even if the will cannot hold one's attention, attention can be held fast when an image that postulates attention is formed. There are various types of images. An image can be a collective image, an imagined visual image, or, under certain circumstances, also a vocal image. It may be a series of words, seen visually and not heard as sound. There are different possibilities. In any event, the attention-stimulating image must possess powers of attraction. Such is the magic of meditation. Therefore, meditation attempts to construct such active images. The person meditating must naturally construct these images himself because only then do they correspond to his nature and possess the power, drawn from his own soul, to hold his attention. The images must, however, be designed as if in accordance to a basic plan, and must take a definite direction. Most of the images are very common, so that they can be used by most everyone, or at least by those with the same cultural background. These images then attract consciousness and, therefore, concentrate attention. And as these images are arranged in a definite manner, a relationship with the centers of life is established. When attention is thus directed to the images, their effects are felt even in physical life, and fluids are produced that circulate in the blood. Blood, which somehow was about to stagnate, is equipped with new life energy, and thereby fresh blood circulation is created. Such exercises are connected with breathing exercises. These, however, are purely technical problems, and do not interest us here. The principal point is the practice of self-analysis; not a self-analysis of reflecting about one's own person, but self-analysis of patient waiting. That which rises from the blood must be seen subtly and gradually. Only thereafter are centers of power of a psychic kind formed, which are suitable to act on the psychic nature, and, through their suggestive power, bring about the internal renewal of the blood.

This is not all. In nature—in the cycle of the day or year—certain forces appear to be present. These from time to time encircle the world like flood waves, although not always to the same degree of strength. The philosopher Mencius, for example, stated that such life-renewing forces are especially strong before daybreak, and they are particularly active after a person has fallen into deep and quiet sleep. For only in such deep sleep is a person sufficiently dissociated to absorb cosmic forces. This dissociation, moreover, can only occur by means of correct exercise. In the state of dissociation one is able to absorb cosmic life forces. Each night a person becomes capable of rinsing away the sediments of day, and refreshed and strengthened, he can meet the new day of life. The technique does not stop here. The human being must consciously enter the stream of time, he must not stand at its banks and contemplate past and future. For then, fear and hope unsettle the soul. Instead, the soul must concentrate its entire life in the present, the here and now, allowing to disappear what must disappear, and allowing to approach what must approach. Then the heart resembles a mirror, and, free of dust, reflects the things as they come and go, always evoking the correct reaction, and never the copied imitation. The endeavor, therefore, is not to suppress the psychic complex of experiences. Rather, one must allow the immediate emergence of the necessary reaction so that all poisonous forces of such impressions can be eliminated.

Mencius sees the soul's peace, active here as the force of life, in as many ways as possible. Everything depends on man. And since, according to Mencius, peace of the soul is also possible on low levels, all these different ways have one thing in common, which is that we cannot suffer the accumulation of unpleasant psychic content. Everything must be always quickly equalized. Unequalized tensions form repressions, which act as obstructions in the unconscious, so that the soul cannot reach the energy sources of strength present in nature that are necessary to breathe freely in constant renewal.

This is the Chinese concept of how life should be prolonged. In addition, there are also certain rules concerning body training, which we might regard as equivalent to our modern sports, were it not for the fact that the Chinese see the issue as basically different. Body exercises in China do not serve the end of establishing an athletic record. To the contrary, physical exercise thus understood would have been considered as wasting life, because outer goals that are not rooted in the body, but in vague opinions of the people, use up disproportionate amounts of physical and of psychic energies. However, aside from this, physical exercises were cultivated in China, but they did not emphasize as their purpose the material What, but the How. Harmony was the highest goal, and achievement was not measured with a yardstick. In archery it was enough for the arrow to hit the center; it did not need to penetrate the leather disc also. For, as Confucius pointed out, in shooting it is important to hit the target, no matter whether the leather skin is pierced or not. Similarly, physical exercise is a part of the endeavor to prolong life, but only in the sense of harmoniously training the body toward goals inherent in that body. Hence, what is to be achieved is the avoidance of a premature death, and not to die any sooner than allotted by the strength of life. Die we must in any event.

The Chinese conceive of life with limits in accordance with nature. These are the "heavenly years" that one is permitted to reach, as long as life is not obstructed. Life, therefore, is thought of as expanding in time, with a beginning and with an end. We cannot say that life is predetermined. However, the abundance, the constancy, and also the rhythm of life are stipulated from the very beginning, as perhaps an entire curve may be calculated from its first three points. Thus physical life is understood as something thoroughly unified. Death is not accident, for nature has set a limit to each life that corresponds both to the vitality and the rhythm of the particular life that has entered space and time. This is neither fortunate nor unfortunate; it is a fact, as for example, the three-dimensional expansion of our spatial life is an accepted fact. To be sure, there may be people who are unhappy because they are not taller or slimmer, but are reconciled to such inconveniences without turning them into problems. Similarly, the duration of physical life is not really a problem, provided it is properly understood.

The issue that becomes a problem, however, is that I want eternity. The body is finite, but the body's finite state is not an unpleasant experience. It dies when the time comes. Yet the body has, as it were, an underside; it has consciousness and imagines death before it dies. Since time immemorial it is precisely this idea of death that has occupied human beings, and perhaps has turned into one of the strongest historical forces. If we visualize all that has been produced by the idea of death, it is overwhelming. Man

built, as a result, pyramids; and he produced religious
and political systems. Man waged wars and fought
battles, and he annihilated millions of people. The
almost geological proportions of this idea are certainly apparent when we consider that pyramids and
other such things were caused by the idea of death
and man's aversion to transitoriness.

What is to be done? One of China's traditions very
boldly dismantles, as it were, the psyche, in order to
see what can be done. Thus Chuang Tzu developed a
philosophy that advocates standing aside and observing the flux of phenomena. His I is no longer limited
to his body, but has become all-encompassing.

But this does not solve the problem. Insofar as we
are dealing not only with an excess of emotion, but
with the security of a position, it is necessary to separate the I from the body. On this point all religions
agree. I want life, but wanting to hold on to life, I will
lose it. Precisely by my adhering to life, life will end by
withdrawing from the I. Therefore, the problem in
Chinese tradition is to form a new body within the
temporal body. This is the idea of rebirth, which is
also found in Christianity; specifically in the esoteric
traditions of the first few centuries, now completely
unknown in the Evangelical Church. Rebirth in early
Christianity was not a mere pious phrase. Paul had
very real things in mind when he fought and struggled; when he wanted to be covered and not un-
covered, and he did not fantasize about a new body of
flesh, to be draped over him like a mantle. In China,
too, we find the attempt to form a new body for the I.
But the task is difficult, and requires very thorough
meditation. For the new body should not be a coarse
body of matter, but a body of energy. Concentration
and meditation exercises are to detach energies, in

order to surround the latently present seed-like entelechy. In the final analysis, this is no different from forming the seedgerm in physical matter. For is not the grain of seed the entelechy of the tree, concentrated so that it becomes invisible, which is not to say that it is not matter, because the potentiality to materialize is always present? Concentration is a latent tension of forces. As the seedgerm falls into the earth, the decaying process stimulates a new and appropriate process. Hence, a regressive movement in ultimate concentration promotes the release. Release occurs because the matter surrounding the grain of seed decays. The Chinese attempt a similar process in the psychic realm. A psychic seed is formed and surrounded with physical energy. Thus a concentrated latent force develops that reaches a point where it separates from primary or transitory time.

In China this is expressed in various images. There may be, for example, a sage, deeply submerged in meditation, and in whose heart a small child is formed. The child is nourished, and eventually rises from the brain cavity. This image reproduces the process of death in life. The departure of the higher energies through the upper body apertures, as described in modern terminology, is simply that we are able to reflect life from a secondarily important time, when we can see our entire life before us. And while our energies can retain contact with material existence, we and consciousness can separate from this life. Thus we do not reflect life in an ordinary sense, but in a preeminently strong sense, saturated by meditation. The process may even be gradually intensified. After all, we do not only live in one time, but we live, as it were, in an onion of different time shells. For example, I am aware of seeing this chair. However, by moving my subject one stratum back, I can take this chair-seeing subject as object, that is, I watch myself see the chair. I can go one step further and observe how I am watching myself see the chair. Yes, this can be continued indefinitely, and is entirely dependent on the individual's psychic strength, on his ability to concentrate, and how far upward he is able to push the process. Some Chinese meditation practices go very far in their uniting the subject's ability to concentrate with making conscious the sense-denominators present in the ego-monad. This process is pictorially represented as if the person in meditation at first separates from within himself the I that is above time. Thereafter five emanations are sent forth, and these, in turn, release five human reflections. Taken as a picture, this looks very peculiar. But, in fact, it signifies a series-like process in time of separation of the I from the material body that exists at first alone.

Strict and serious contemplative work is demanded here. However, contemplation is not simply an intellectual process, as we are accustomed to think of it in the West. Thought and existence are to us two irreconcilable opposites. Chinese thought, on the other hand, regards contemplation as a process that is concentrated in such a way as to be effective in the world of existence. The Chinese character for "thinking" is written with field and heart, consciousness beneath the field—hence a field where consciousness is active. The characters for "thought" are tones that originate in consciousness. They are, as it were, tonal images that emerge from the consciously worked-over field. We are, of course, dealing here with concepts and imageries that only with great difficulty attempt to indicate their meaning. (Similarly, our own philosophical concepts are also figurative and very inaccurate.) At this point, we are concerned with the very practical task of becoming independent of life while alive—not only theoretically, but practically as well. Such independence is reached when, like a seed, we form this something that Goethe calls an entelechy. This is a power with a definite rhythm and with a definite direction, and with the attribute of being closed within itself. An entelechy in this sense is like a small self-contained world system. All of Chinese thinking—Confucianism, Taoism, as well as Buddhism—contains the idea that in the course of life, man will shape harmoniously those psychic and physical predispositions that he received as capital assets by unifying them and giving them form from within a center.

He who succeeds in this has enormous power. But the question is whether one can succeed. It is entirely possible that a person will not manage to keep together the soul entities united within him. Rather, one or another of these entities may at times escape and wander about independently in the dream world. When this happens, a person makes contact with departed ghosts, or with ghosts of a nonhuman nature. But in China, such matters are less questions of belief than they are the subject of manifold entertainment in fairy tales.

Hence, such incidents occur only infrequently, for the goal is always the unification of the soul by means of consistent practice. It is presupposed that this self-contained entelechy is a state which, though potentially higher, is in the present stage of development an as yet undeveloped state. As a potentially higher state, it views the past and the future; it is intuitive and, therefore, superior to intellect. And this seems a strange idea indeed: the higher and intuitive aspect must be cultivated and formed by consciousness, which in relationship to it is inferior. This means that the divine in man—if we want to use this expression here—requires the guidance of the human element, or consciousness, for its development. The higher aspects in man are taught and formed by means of guidance of consciousness. The Chinese take this very seriously. That which involuntarily gushes and bubbles forth from the unconscious is in Europe frequently, or at least at times, considered as a sign of special genius. In China it is considered wasted power; undeveloped births of eternal life, which must scatter again, because they are not concentrated in themselves.

The issue is therefore to acquaint oneself with the state after death, while still in life. The occasion for this is provided in sleep. According to Chuang Tzu, the spirit wanders in sleep, and in sleep the soul dwells in the liver. By this he means that the soul in sleep is not in the brain or in consciousness, but in the vegetative realm. In fact, deep sleep, or the complete absence of consciousness, is a state very similar to that after death. Therefore, it is important to cultivate one's dreams, because by cultivating dreams one trains for life after death. The sage no longer dreams; he is not subject to these images that form chaotically—visually or accoustically—in the imagination. He is in accord with world happening, both in sleep or in deep sleep, so that these last timid vestiges of consciousness fall away from him. Like very clear water that no longer shows images, and where everything is seen clearly down to the bottom, his sleep also is truly pure and transparent.

Next to the physical and psychic I, we have now a third, spiritual, and highest I. That the psychic I can develop so extensively is possible only because of the third and highest I which, in distinction to the individual, psychic I, is universal. Bound by neither body nor psyche, it is the great I of mankind, the world-I. When the psychic entelechy vibrates together with the rhythm of this world-I, so that the experience of I is transposed into it—not only momentarily but for a deep and strengthening time of rest—the state after death can be experienced without fear.

The task of life, therefore, is to prepare for death. But not in the sense of accounting for a certain number of good deeds, which enable one to enter heaven. Instead, the preparation consists in creating a state which, separated from finite existence, represents infinity, and that one centers one's I in this infinite and eternal state. This is, as it were, a flight from the world. Of course, there is also a point when this I must detach itself. This is dying. But such dying is tied in with a new becoming, and guards against continued dying. The idea is similar to that of birth. Indeed, birth is a mighty revolution, when heaven and earth displace one another for the sake of the human being. Heaven and earth change places. A new rebirth is, therefore, once more a spiritual recentering. Heaven and earth change places again; what previously was above is now below; and what was below is now above, thus making possible a new form of existence, which is eternal. Once a person has reached this standpoint he will fear death no longer. Instead, he will regard death as sleep, as a physiological process, common to all men, which is easily managed if not regarded seriously as process. A person's position in life will also assume an essentially different perspective, because now he is, as it were, reborn. When confronted with matters eternal, he will maintain seriousness, while the flow of temporal matters will not disturb him—these can no longer occupy him deeply. To the Taoist this means assuming an ironical and humorous attitude and laughing about all mortal doings. But to the Confucian, it means assuming an attitude of independent aloofness, which enables him to descend from highest heights to a position where he must fulfill all duties connected with this position. He can take this course not because he is inherently virtuous, nor because he desires merit, but simply because this way of acting in life corresponds to his nature. Where he stands is now no longer significant. There is no more need to cross over into the other world; although he continues to live in this world, he is already there. This beyond, however, is neither temporally nor spatially separated from the world, but is Tao, which uniformly penetrates all existence and becoming. It is seriousness and sanctity that makes death appear not as something terrible; it is that which makes life into eternity.[10]

Notes

Introduction

All references to the text of the *I Ching* are taken from *The I Ching or Book of Changes*, the Richard Wilhelm translation, rendered into English by Cary F. Baynes, third edition (Princeton and London, 1967; Bollingen Series XIX).

1. Chen Shih-chuan, "How to Form a Hexagram and Consult the *I Ching*," *Journal of the American Oriental Society*, 92 no. 2 (April-June 1972), 239.

2. The first essay was presented as two lectures in the fall of 1929. The second essay consists of three lectures that were given in 1926 at the Goethehaus in Frankfurt, and the third essay was also delivered as three lectures in 1927. The last essay is two lectures from the fall of 1928. All lectures were first published in *Chinesisch-Deutscher Almanach* between 1928 and 1930. They were later included in a collection of essays and lectures: Richard Wilhelm, *Der Mensch und das Sein* (Jena, 1931) and published the same year separately under the title of *Wandlung und Dauer* (Jena). The volume used for this translation is a reissue of *Wandlung und Dauer, die Weisheit des I Ging* (Dusseldorf-Cologne, 1956).

3. Jung's interests are well known. See, for example, his lengthy commentary on *Das Geheimnis der Goldenen Blüte*, translated by Richard Wilhelm (Munich, 1929). For a provocative article treating Jung's views, see R. C. Zaehner, "A New Buddhism and a New Tao," in R. C. Zaehner, ed., *The Concise Encyclopedia of Living Faiths* (Boston, 1967), pp. 402-412. See also Martin Buber's contribution to the fall meeting of the China Institute in *Chinesisch-Deutscher Almanach für das Jahr Gi Si 1929/30*. Or his much earlier introduction to a German translation of P'u Sung-ling's Liao Chai stories, *Chinesische Geister- und Liebesgeschichten* (Frankfurt, 1911).

4. Hellmut Wilhelm, *Change, Eight Lectures on the I Ching*, translated by Cary F. Baynes (New York and London, 1960; Bollingen Series LXII), p. x. Italics in the original.

5. The seizure of Chiao-chou Bay and the port of Tsingtao established the German sphere of influence in Shantung province. This, together with the signing of the treaty in March 1898, precipitated a scramble for concessions among the Powers. See John E. Schrecker, *Imperialism and Nationalism, Germany in Shantung* (Cambridge, Mass., 1971). For the German missionary educational effort in Shantung, see p. 243.

6. The above account is based on the biography by Wilhelm's widow, Salome Wilhelm, *Richard Wilhelm, der Geistige Mittler zwischen China und Europa* (Dusseldorf-Cologne, 1956).

7. Chen, "How to Form a Hexagram" justifiably points out that the divinatory procedure influences the understanding of the *I Ching* text. The procedure given by Wilhelm (and for that matter by other Western translators) dates from the Sung dynasty (960-1278) and is, therefore, staunchly Confucian. Wilhelm based his translation on the *Chou I Che Chung*, a collection of Sung commentaries by scholars of the Ch'ing dynasty (1644-1912), of the K'ang Hsi period (1662-1722).

8. Wilhelm was at Peking University shortly after the May Fourth Movement of 1919, and would not have been oblivious to the revolutionary intellectual currents with its critical and anti-Confucian overtones.

9. Wilhelm, *Richard Wilhelm*, pp. 371, 314-316.

10. Richard Wilhelm, "Die Bedeutung des Morgenländischen Geistes für die Abendländische Erneuerung," in *Der Mensch und das Sein*, pp. 114-115, 124-129.

11. Wilhelm, *Richard Wilhelm*, p. 340. This, from his talk at the opening of the China Institute in 1925.

12. Joseph R. Levenson, "The Genesis of 'Confucian China and Its Modern Fate,'" in L. P. Curtis, Jr., ed., *The Historian's Workshop* (New York, 1970), p. 279.

13. Wilhelm, *Richard Wilhelm*, pp. 340-341.

14. Levenson, "Genesis," p. 287.

15. Wilhelm, *Richard Wilhelm*, p. 345.

16. H. G. Creel, *The Origins of Statecraft in China, The Western Chou Empire* (Chicago and London, 1970), I, 445-447, and note 4, p. 445. See also J. Y. Lee, "Some Reflections on the Authorship of the *I Ching*," *Numen*, 17 (December 1970), 201, who distinguishes four formative stages, in which the first is that of divination.

17. *The I Ching*, pp. xiv-xv.

18. Herbert A. Giles, tr., *Chuang Tzu, Taoist Philosopher and Chinese Mystic* (London, 1961), p. 151. This is chapter 14 of the *Chuang Tzu*. Presumably Confucius informs Lao Tzu that he "arranged" the six classics: Poetry, History, Rites, Music, Changes, and Spring and Autumn Annals.

19. Gerald W. Swanson, "The Great Treatise: Commentary Tradition to the Book of Changes," Ph.D. dissertation, University of Washington, 1974, p. 408.

20. See, for example, Li Ching-ch'un, *Chou-I che-hsüeh chi-ch'i pien-cheng-fa yin-su* (The philosophy of the *Changes* and its dialectic factor) (Tsinan, 1961). For a listing of materials on this topic, see Wing-tsit Chan, *Chinese Philosophy, 1949-1963: An Annotated Bibliography of Mainland China Publications* (Honolulu, 1967). Hellmut Wilhelm in his preface to *The I Ching*, p. xvii, remarks that "the two issues which engendered nationwide discussions were the ethical system of Confucius and the *Book of Changes*."

21. *Wen Wu*, no. 7 (1974), pp. 42-43, and no. 9 (1974), pp. 40-57.

22. *Ku Shih Pien* (Discussions on ancient Chinese history), edited by Ku Chieh-kang and others (Hong Kong, 1963), 3, 1-308. Among the contributors to these investigations were Ku Chieh-kang, Ch'ien Hsüan-t'ung, Hu Shih, and Ch'ien Mu.

23. Hellmut Wilhelm, *Sinn des I Ging* (Dusseldorf-Cologne, 1972), p. 110.

24. *The I Ching*, p. xxiv. See also Wayne McEvilly, "Synchronicity and the *I Ching*," *Philosophy East and West*, 18 (1968), 137-144.

25. James R. Hightower, *The Poetry of T'ao Ch'ien* (Oxford, 1970), p. 6.

Opposition and Fellowship

1. The *Doctrine of the Mean* (Chung Yung) is traditionally attributed to Tzu-ssu, the grandson of Confucius. The book, however, seems to be a combination of texts, some of which apparently date from the Ch'in dynasty (221-206 B.C.) or from shortly thereafter. The *Doctrine of the Mean* is one of the Confucian classics.

2. Translation according to Arthur Waley, *The Way and Its Power, A Study of the Tao Te Ching and Its Place in Chinese Thought* (New York, 1958), chapter 42.

3. See *The I Ching*, p. 268.

4. In the Wilhelm-Baynes translation this passage is slightly different. "That the holy sages turned their faces to the south while they gave ear to the meaning of the universe, means that in ruling they turned toward what is light." *The I Ching*, p. 269.

5. The Duke of Chou was the son of King Wen, founder of the Chou dynasty (1122-221 B.C.). After the death of King Wu, who is credited with subduing the Shang dynasty (traditional dates, 1766-1122 B.C.), he became a most powerful political figure in his capacity of regent for the minor heir to the throne, King Ch'eng. Tradition assigns to him the preeminent position of creator of Chou culture. He is described as a scholar and philosopher—an intellectual giant—as well as a capable statesman and ruler.

6. *Lun Yü* (The Analects), 1, 4. For the English translation of this and subsequent references from the Analects see Arthur Waley, tr., *The Analects of Confucius* (London, 1956).

7. English translation according to E. A. Bowring, *The Poems of Goethe, Translated in the Original Metres* (New York, 1882), p. 242. The poem is dated 1815. This section was translated by Jane A. Pratt, "The Circulation of Events: as Depicted in the Chinese Book of Changes," *Spring*, 1961, pp. 91-108.

8. See Introduction, above, p. xii and p. 167, note 2.

9. The text here consists of several combined commentaries. See *The I Ching*, p. 574.

10. Wilhelm's statement and terminology must be understood within the context of the twenties and the strong humanist rejection of imposed and possibly successful uniformity.

11. Max Scheler (1874-1928) was a leading German philosopher, whose broad interests included ethics, religion, psychology, anthropology, and politics. Wilhelm and Scheler apparently shared ideas, for when offered a teaching post in Frankfurt, Scheler was pleased to be in close proximity to Wilhelm's China Institute. See John R. Staude, *Max Scheler, An Intellectual Portrait* (New York and London, 1967), p. 249.

12. Friedrich Schiller, "Das Ideal und das Leben," *Sämtliche Werke* (Munich, 1973), Vol. 1.

13. *Lun Yü*, 14, 41.

The Spirit of Art According
to the Book of Changes

1. In his poem "Dauer im Wechsel" (Constancy in Change), which Richard Wilhelm used as a motif in the next chapter, Goethe stated clearly that the well-formed image, "das gegliederte Gebilde," is subject to relentless change.

2. The German word *Linie*, or line, does not refer to a line of a trigram or of a hexagram, but stands for the Chinese concept *wen*. Depending on the context, this may mean the line markings of a stone, particularly jade.

3. *Lun Yü*, 3, 8.

4. Ibid., 6, 16.

5. Goethe, "Chinese-German Times of the Year and Day," no. 11, *Gedenkausgabe*, Sämtliche Gedichte (Zurich, 1962), II, 54.

6. The implied meaning here is grace mellowed by wine, a condition that also has its dangers. See *The I Ching*, pp. 92, 498.

7. Goethe's poem is dated 1827.

8. T'ao Yüan-ming (T'ao Ch'ien) lived from 365 to 427. He retired early from official life and lived in the country.

Much of his poetry deals with nature and country living, and he often refers to song and music. See Hightower, *The Poetry of T'ao Ch'ien*.

9. See the final verse at the end of "Faust," part II, which expresses this idea.

10. *Lieh Tzu*, 5, 13. For the English translation, see A. C. Graham, *The Book of Lieh Tzu* (London, 1960), pp. 109-110.

11. This episode, which illustrates Confucius' relationship to music, is recorded in *K'ung Tzu Chia Yü* (The School Sayings of Confucius), 35, 1. Parallel text in Szu-ma Ch'ien, *Shih Chi* (Historical Records), 47.

12. Neither the Chinese *li* nor the German word *Sitte* used by Wilhelm has an English equivalent. Various terms have been used by English translators, the most recent being "rites and propriety" by Noah Edward Fehl, *Li, Rites and Propriety in Literature and Life* (Hong Kong, 1971). Within the context of this essay, proper conduct seems appropriate and should be understood as including conduct proper to spiritual, ethical, social, or ceremonial aspects.

13. The poem is entitled "Ein Andres," and follows the poem "Memento." Both date from 1813.

14. Goethe made repeated reference to the two enemies, fear and hope. See, for example, "Iphigenie auf Tauris" (1786), act III, scene 1: neither fear nor hope will save Clytemnestra, says Iphigenie; or "Faust," part II, act 1, where fear and hope appear personified and are described as linked together.

15. *Lun Yü*, 2, 3. Wilhelm's translation reproduced here is a free rendering of, "Lead them [the people] by regulations, order them with punishments, and the people will flee and have no conscience."

16. This is a fanciful short story by the youthful Goethe. Aside from other complications of the plot, a child pacifies a dangerous lion with music and love.

Constancy in Change

1. English version according to Bowring, *The Poems of Goethe*, p. 79.

2. Wilhelm refers here to the so-called Well-field system (*ching-t'ien*), mentioned in *Mencius*, 3, 3, 19. Eight private squares of field were thought to be situated around a central public square. Each private square was cultivated by one family, and the public square was tilled in common. Whether or not such a land division in fact existed is open to question.

3. This line is from Goethe's poem "Allerdings," dated 1820. The final lines read: "Nature has neither seed nor shell/ It is everything at once./ Foremost examine yourself,/ Whether you are seed or shell."

4. Graham, *The Book of Lieh Tzu*, pp. 28-29. Little is known about Lieh Tzu. He may have lived around 398 B.C., and was a native of the state of Cheng.

5. Chou Hsin is considered to be the last ruler of the Shang dynasty. A seductive concubine supported his brutality and sensual excesses, according to Chinese traditional history, so that he neglected affairs of state. King Wen's son, King Wu, attacked the Shang armies, who were no match for Chou military might. The 700,000 men of the Shang armies were destroyed or dispersed, and Chou Hsin immolated himself in his imperial residence.

6. The poem is dated September 3, 1783. It is an exquisite statement on self-denial and waiting, because the certainty of the goal is not doubted.

7. The image of the eternally weaving maiden occurs in Goethe's poem "Antipirrhema," dated 1820.

8. The German term used is "Die Entwerdung." As this section makes clear, depersonalization should be understood in its broadest possible meaning; not as negation or illusion, but depersonalization toward the goal of realizing oneself within humanity as a whole.

9. See Goethe, "Urworte-Orphisch, Dämon," dated 1817.

10. *Mencius* 6, 15, 1.

11. See above, p. 172, note 12

12. Hexagram 9, nine in the third place. *The I Ching*, p. 433.

Death and Renewal

1. *Lun Yü*, 11, 11.

2. *K'ung Tzu Chia Yü*, 8, 17. The first ten sections of this work were translated by R. P. Kramers, *K'ung Tzu Chia Yü* (The School Sayings of Confucius) (Leiden, 1950).

3. Richard Wilhelm's translation in this place differs somewhat from that of the Wilhelm-Baynes version. Here he wanted to introduce the concepts of *hun* and *p'o* (animus and anima) discussed below in note 5. The outgoing and returning spirits, "Geister und Dämone," are *shen* and *kuei*, also discussed in note 5. See *The I Ching*, p. 294.

4. The *Book of Documents* (*Shang Shu* or *Shu Ching*) ranks among the oldest of the Confucian classics. It contains heterogeneous historical materials on the early history of the Chou dynasty.

5. Wilhelm uses the Jungian terms, animus and anima, for what in China are considered the two component parts of the soul, *hun* and *p'o*. *Hun* is the more spiritual or yang part, which derives its power from the fact that it is a *shen* by nature, and hence allied with benevolent spirits. *P'o* is the yin component, which, if not placated by proper burial and sacrifice, may turn into a *kuei*, a ghost or devil, with malevolent tendencies. The *p'o* resides in the grave (or earth); the *hun* dwells in higher regions.

6. Hsü Chih-mo (1895-1931), no doubt one of the foremost poets of the twenties, was in America and Europe, where his creative career was molded by Western writers. A faithful admirer of Tagore, Hsü was his interpreter and companion when Tagore visited China in 1924. Hsü died tragically in November 1931 in an airplane crash. For a selection of his poetry see Hsü Kai-yu, ed., *Twentieth Century Chinese Poetry* (New York, 1964), pp. 69-96.

7. Yüeh Fei (1103-1141) was a patriotic military leader, who attempted to save the empire from the northern invaders. He was not successful, and was murdered in the course of court intrigues. For a biographical sketch see Hellmut Wilhelm, "From Myth to Myth: The Case of Yüeh

Fei's Biography," in Arthur F. Wright, ed., *Confucianism and Chinese Civilization* (New York, 1964), pp. 211-226.

8. Translation from the *Tao Te Ching* is according to Waley, *The Way and Its Power*, chapters 16 and 6.

9. His dates are given as 365-290 B.C. His philosophical works are translated by Burton Watson, *The Complete Works of Chuang Tzu* (New York, 1964).

10. This chapter was earlier translated by Jane A. Pratt, "Death and Renewal," *Spring*, 1962, pp. 20-44.

Index

Names of hexagrams and trigrams are given in English. The name of each hexagram is followed by its number in parentheses. Both hexagrams and trigrams, when accompanied by a portion of text from the *Book of Changes*, will have the reference in **boldface** type.

LIBRARY OF CONGRESS CATALOGING
IN PUBLICATION DATA

Wilhelm, Richard, 1873-1930.
  Lectures on the I ching.

  (Bollingen Series; XIX, 2)
  Translation of Wandlung und Dauer.
  Includes bibliographical references and index.
  1. I ching—Addresses, essays, lectures.
I. Title.
PL.2464.Z7W55513   299'.5128'2   78-84027
ISBN 0-691-09902-2
ISBN 0-691-01872-3 (pbk.)